Easy Cooking with Your
NINJA® FOODI

Easy Cooking with Your NINJA® FOODI

75 Recipes for Incredible One-Pot Meals in Half the Time

KRISTY BERNARDO

Author of *Weeknight Cooking with Your Instant Pot®* and founder of The Wicked Noodle

Photography by Becky Winkler

PAGE STREET
PUBLISHING CO.

PAGE STREET
PUBLISHING CO.

FOR LARA

THANK YOU FOR YOUR ENCOURAGEMENT,
UNCONDITIONAL FRIENDSHIP AND
SO MANY GOOD TIMES!

CONTENTS

INTRODUCTION

If you're familiar with my other cookbooks, you know that I've been pressure cooking for quite a few years. Pressure cooking is a method that transformed the way I cook, and it's the main way I get meals on our table these days. At first, I hesitated to try the newest pressure cooker on the market. Yet the moment I unboxed my Ninja Foodi, my skepticism began to fall away. The thought of being able to saute my ingredients, then pressure cook them in the same machine, then broil the top without the need to transfer my food to the oven was almost unbelievable to me! I was cautiously optimistic, but it turned out that the Ninja Foodi has transformed the way I cook for the better.

The Ninja Foodi is a solid, well-made and well-designed machine. It has multiple temperature settings for sauteing. It can bake, it can broil, it can pressure cook and it can air fry. It can even be used as a dehydrator! And it does it all very, very well. Breaded chicken that is typically deep-fried turns out just as good when air-fried, plus there are fewer calories and fat. During the hot summer months, there will no longer be a need to turn on your oven since you can bake just about anything right in your Foodi. Even desserts turn out well.

The recipes I've shared in this book are all family favorites that we've enjoyed time and time again. My hope is that this book becomes well-worn with use and that you use your Ninja Foodi as often as we use ours!

K Bernardo

TIPS & TRICKS FOR THE NINJA FOODI

The recipes in this book have been written and tested for a 6.5-quart (6-L) Ninja Foodi. Be aware that if you use a different size, you may need to adjust the cooking times.

Here are a few tips and tricks I've learned from using my Foodi:

When using the Bake/Roast function, always check your food earlier than you would if you were using the oven. The Foodi works similarly to a convection/fan oven and will often be done much sooner than you may be used to.

If you're in a rush, use hot water when using the Pressure Cook function. It will slightly speed up the process of coming to pressure.

When using the Pressure Cook function, the Foodi will automatically switch to the Keep Warm setting after the time is up. This feature is very convenient if you have to run out for a short time or you're busy working on something else. Start the Foodi and come back to a finished meal when you're ready!

When using the Air Crisp function, cooking in small batches almost always works best. Place your food in a single layer, leaving a small amount of space around each piece of food to ensure it cooks evenly on all sides. Some recipes also work best if you flip the food halfway through cooking time.

If you have leftovers you'd like to reheat, try using the Steam function. I typically either wrap my food in aluminum foil or place it in a heat-safe container and cover it with aluminum foil, then steam it for 5 to 12 minutes. You'll love being able to reheat your leftovers without using the microwave or the oven.

Another convenient feature of the Foodi is the timer. This allows you to set a specific amount of time before you want the cooking process to begin. I most often use this feature when I have to leave my house at 3 p.m. for after-school pickup but won't be home until 6 or 7 p.m. I'll delay the cooking process for 1 to 2 hours, depending on how long it will take to cook (and assuming the ingredients I'm using can sit out for that long). Then, when the Foodi finishes cooking, it automatically switches to the Keep Warm setting so it will be ready for dinner as soon as we walk through the door.

Although many of the Foodi's components, such as the cooking pot, can be cleaned in the dishwasher, I recommend handwashing everything. The cooking pot is nonstick and cleans very easily. It's worth the extra minute or two to keep everything in top-notch condition.

The Foodi isn't made for outdoor use, but it would be a great choice for a dorm room or to use during hot months when you don't want to turn on the oven. I use mine almost daily in the summertime!

ULTIMATE ONE-POT MEALS

Sheet-pan dinners and one-skillet recipes are very popular, but none can compare to the ease and versatility of one-pot meals made in the Ninja Foodi. Where else can you saute, pressure cook, bake and broil (just to name a few) all with the same machine? Not to mention it won't heat your house the way an oven will, making it even more appreciated in hot weather. Try a flavorful jambalaya or an easy-yet-flavorful mulligatawny soup. Or keep it classic with a hearty beef stew with the biscuits baked on top, right in your Foodi!

My Three Favorites

CLASSIC FRENCH ONION SOUP

SERVES 8

Functions Used
Sear/Saute, Pressure Cook, Broil

1 tbsp (15 ml) extra-virgin olive oil

5 to 6 Vidalia onions, sliced

1 shallot, sliced

1 tsp fresh thyme leaves

⅓ cup (79 ml) dry red wine

4 cups (946 ml) beef broth or stock

2 tsp (9 g) light brown sugar

1 tsp Worcestershire sauce

1 bay leaf

1 tsp coarse salt

¼ tsp freshly ground black pepper

8 slices from a French baguette

¾ cup (91 g) shredded Gruyère or Swiss cheese

One of the wonderful things about the Ninja Foodi is that you can broil the tops of foods without the need to transfer them to the oven, making this classic French onion soup a perfect choice. Pressure cook the soup for just 20 minutes, then broil the cheesy bread topping all in one pot!

Press **Sear/Saute** and set the heat to **Med–Low**. Allow the Foodi to preheat for **5 minutes**. Add the oil to the pot and when it's shimmering, add the onions and shallot. Cook for about **15 minutes**, stirring frequently, until the onions are lightly browned. Stir in the thyme leaves and cook for **1 minute**.

Add the wine and allow it to reduce by half, stirring frequently, about **5 minutes**. Add the beef broth, brown sugar, Worcestershire, bay leaf, salt and pepper. Place the pressure lid onto the pot and make sure the valve is set to **Seal**. Press **Pressure** and set to **HI**. Set the timer to **20 minutes**, then press **Start**.

When the time is up, allow the pressure to release naturally. Carefully remove the pressure lid, then remove the bay leaf and stir the soup. Place the bread slices on top of the soup, then sprinkle the bread with the cheese. Close the crisping lid and select **Broil**. Set the timer to **2 minutes**, then press **Start**. When the time is up, open the lid and scoop the soup with the cheesy bread into bowls.

MUSTARD & THYME
BEEF STEW WITH BISCUITS

SERVES 6

Functions Used
Sear/Saute, Pressure Cook,
Bake/Roast

3 tbsp (45 ml) extra-virgin
olive oil

2 lbs (908 g) beef stew meat,
cut into 1-inch (2.5-cm) pieces

1 medium onion, chopped

2 celery ribs, chopped

4 carrots, sliced into 1-inch
(2.5-cm) pieces

3 tbsp (24 g) all-purpose flour

1 lb (454 g) red potatoes, cut
into bite-sized pieces

1 (14.5-oz [411-g]) can
fire-roasted diced tomatoes,
with liquid

2 cups (474 ml) beef broth or
stock

1 tsp dry mustard

½ tsp dried thyme

½ tsp salt

½ tsp freshly ground black
pepper

1 (16.3-oz [462-g]) can ready-
to-bake buttermilk biscuits
(8 biscuits total)

The flavor combination of mustard and thyme turns a simple beef stew into something company-worthy! Add the fact that you can bake the biscuits right on top—all in the same pot—and this easy stew becomes an instant family favorite.

Press **Sear/Saute** and set the heat to **Medium**. Allow the Foodi to preheat for **5 minutes**.

Add the oil to the pot and when it's shimmering, add the stew meat. Cook until browned, about **5 minutes**.

Add the onion, celery and carrots, and cook for about **5 minutes**, stirring occasionally. Add the flour and cook for about **1 minute**, stirring frequently. Add the potatoes, tomatoes, broth, mustard and thyme to the pot. Place the pressure lid onto the pot and make sure the valve is set to **Seal**. Press **Pressure** and set to **HI**. Set the timer to **30 minutes**, then press **Start**.

When the time is up, carefully release the pressure by turning the valve to **Vent**. Remove the pressure lid, stir the stew and season with the salt and pepper.

Place all of the biscuits on top of the stew in a single layer. Close the crisping lid. Press **Bake/Roast** and set the temperature to **350°F (177°C)** and the timer to **15 minutes**. Press **Start**. Bake for **15 minutes**, or until the biscuits are browned and cooked through.

MULLIGATAWNY SOUP

SERVES 8

Functions Used
Sear/Saute, Pressure Cook

2 tbsp (30 ml) extra-virgin olive oil

½ large sweet onion, chopped

3 carrots, chopped

2 large celery ribs, chopped

1 large green apple, peeled, cored and grated

2 tbsp (15 g) all-purpose flour

2 tbsp (15 g) yellow curry powder, plus more if desired

8 cups (1.8 L) reduced-sodium chicken stock or broth

1 cup (211 g) orzo or white rice

4–6 cups (560–840 g) cooked, diced chicken (I use the meat from a whole rotisserie chicken)

½ tsp coarse salt

¼ tsp freshly ground black pepper

If you love curry and a simple chicken soup, then this easy dish will be your go-to! Flavored with yellow curry and the sweetness from an apple, this comforting soup will make an easy weeknight meal extra delicious. Normally you'd simmer this soup for at least an hour, but the Foodi cuts your time by more than half!

Press **Sear/Saute** and set the heat to **Medium**. Allow the Foodi to preheat for **5 minutes**.

Add the oil to the pot and when it's shimmering, add the onion, carrots and celery. Cook for about **5 minutes**, stirring frequently. Stir in the grated apple and cook for **2 minutes**.

Whisk in the flour and curry powder and cook for **1 minute**, or until it's all thoroughly combined. Add 1 cup (237 ml) of the broth, whisking constantly until the mixture is smooth, then add the remaining broth. Add the orzo, chicken, salt and pepper, then stir well.

Place the pressure lid onto the pot and make sure the valve is set to **Seal**. Press **Pressure** and set to **HI**. Set the timer to **20 minutes**, then press **Start**.

When the time is up, carefully release the pressure by turning the valve to **Vent**. Carefully remove the pressure lid and stir the soup. Taste the soup and adjust any seasonings you'd like, adding more curry powder if you prefer a stronger flavor.

CREAMY MAC & CHEESE WITH BACON BREADCRUMBS

SERVES 4 TO 6

Functions Used
Sear/Saute, Pressure Cook, Broil

The combination of cheesy, creamy macaroni with a buttery bacon breadcrumb topping in this quick and simple recipe is to die for! The crispy top is a wonderful texture contrast to the creamy pasta, and the Ninja Foodi makes fast work of it all. The whole family will love this one!

8 slices bacon, sliced crosswise into ½-inch (1-cm) pieces

1½ cups (84 g) panko breadcrumbs

2 tbsp (30 g) butter, melted

1 tsp hot sauce

2 tsp (10 g) yellow mustard

1 tsp coarse salt

4 cups (946 ml) water

1 lb (454 g) dry macaroni

1–2 cups (237–473 ml) whole milk

1 lb (454 g) sharp Cheddar, shredded

½ cup (40 g) shaved Parmesan

½ tsp coarse salt

½ tsp freshly ground black pepper

Press **Sear/Saute** and set the heat to **Medium**. Allow the Foodi to preheat for **5 minutes**.

Add the bacon and cook, stirring occasionally, until the bacon is crisp, about **8 to 10 minutes**.

Remove the bacon with a slotted spoon. Holding the pot with a hot pad, discard the grease from the pan and thoroughly wipe the inside with a paper towel. Crumble the bacon and mix it with the breadcrumbs and melted butter. Set aside.

Mix the hot sauce, mustard, salt and water in the Foodi pot. Pour in the macaroni and make sure it's all submerged. Place the pressure lid onto the pot and make sure the valve is set to **Seal**. Press **Pressure** and set to **HI**. Set the timer to **4 minutes**, then press **Start**.

When the time is up, carefully release the pressure by turning the valve to **Vent**. Remove the lid and stir the pasta to break it up. Tilt the pan to drain any excess liquid; you can leave a small amount. Add 1 cup (237 ml) of the milk and both cheeses; stir until completely incorporated and the cheese has melted and coated the pasta. Add the remaining milk in increments, if desired, until the sauce is as thick and creamy as you like. Stir in the salt and pepper.

Evenly sprinkle the reserved breadcrumb mixture on top of the mac and cheese. Close the crisping lid and press **Broil**. Set the timer to **2 minutes**, then press **Start**. Check after **1 minute** to see if the topping is browned to your liking, otherwise continue broiling until it's golden brown.

SWEET CORN CAKE ENCHILADA BAKE

SERVES 4

Functions Used
Sear/Saute, Bake/Roast

2 lbs (908 g) ground beef

2 tsp (5 g) chili powder

2½ cups (638 g) enchilada sauce

2 (4-oz [113-g]) cans diced green chiles

2 ears fresh corn, kernels removed and cobs discarded (optional)

2½ cups (283 g) shredded Cheddar cheese

1 (8.5-oz [240-g]) box corn muffin mix (such as Jiffy)

1 egg

¼ cup (60 g) butter, melted

1 (14.5-oz [411-g]) can creamed corn

⅓ cup (64 g) sugar

A large pinch of coarse salt

I've been making sweet corn cake for years, and I was thrilled when I realized I could bake it right on top of my enchilada filling! The fresh corn adds a wonderful texture and flavor, but you can use frozen corn or omit it if you don't have fresh corn on hand. Either way, you'll love this delicious one-pot meal!

Press **Sear/Saute** and set the heat to **Medium**. Allow the Foodi to preheat for **5 minutes**. Add the ground beef and cook, stirring occasionally until no pink remains, about **5 minutes**. Drain off any fat from the pot.

Add the chili powder, enchilada sauce, green chiles and corn kernels (if using). Cook for **3 to 4 minutes**, just until bubbling and hot, stirring occasionally. Stir in the shredded cheese. Turn off the heat.

In a medium-sized mixing bowl, combine the corn muffin mix, egg, melted butter, creamed corn, sugar and salt. Spread the corn mixture over the beef mixture in the pot. Close the crisping lid. Press **Bake/Roast** and set the temperature to **350°F (177°C)** and the timer to **25 minutes**. Press **Start**.

Bake until the corn cake is just a tiny bit jiggly in the center, adding an extra **5 minutes** or so if necessary. Once it's ready, allow it to sit uncovered for **5 to 10 minutes** before serving.

HAM & SWISS FRITTATA

SERVES 4

Functions Used
Sear/Saute, Bake/Roast

2 tsp (10 ml) extra-virgin olive oil

⅓ cup (50 g) chopped onion

12 large eggs

½ cup (118 ml) low-fat milk

1 tsp coarse salt

¼ tsp freshly ground black pepper

2 cups (300 g) cooked, chopped ham

1½ cups (181 g) shredded low-fat Swiss cheese

We're big on breakfast-for-dinner, and a frittata in the Foodi couldn't be easier! Whenever I have leftover ham, I'll make this recipe, but I love it so much that I also buy ham just to make it. It feeds our family of four and makes everyone's bellies happy.

Press **Sear/Saute** and set the heat to **Medium**. Allow the Foodi to preheat for **5 minutes**.

Add the oil to the pot and when it's shimmering, add the onion. Cook until the onion is soft, **4 to 5 minutes**.

Meanwhile, beat the eggs in a medium-sized mixing bowl. Add the milk, salt, pepper, ham and Swiss cheese, and stir well.

Press **Stop** to turn off the heat, then pour the egg mixture over the onions and stir to combine. Close the crisping lid. Press **Bake/Roast** and set the temperature to **390°F (199°C)** and the timer to **15 minutes**. Press **Start**. Cook until the eggs are completely cooked through.

EASY CHEESY BEEF PASTA

SERVES 4 TO 6

Functions Used
Sear/Saute, Pressure Cook

2 lbs (907 g) ground beef

½ medium onion, chopped

3 cloves garlic, minced

2 tsp (10 ml) Worcestershire sauce

1 tbsp (15 g) seasoned salt (such as Lawry's)

¼ tsp freshly ground black pepper

1 tbsp (5 g) dried oregano

1 tbsp (5 g) dried basil

3 cups (710 ml) water

2 cups (210 g) dry macaroni

2 (8-oz [227-g]) cans tomato sauce

2 (14.5-oz [411-g]) cans fire-roasted diced tomatoes, with liquid

1¼ cups (151 g) shredded Cheddar cheese

This cheesy pasta is what I make for my kids when we get home late from after-school activities and everyone is tired. They always gobble it up, plus the leftovers are even more delicious the next day.

Press **Sear/Saute** and set the heat to **Medium**. Allow the Foodi to preheat for **5 minutes**. Add the ground beef and onion to the pot and cook until no pink remains in the beef, about **5 minutes**. Add the garlic, Worcestershire, seasoned salt, pepper, dried oregano and dried basil and cook for **1 minute**, stirring frequently.

Add the water and macaroni to the pot. Stir well and scrape up any browned bits on the bottom of the pot. Add the tomato sauce and diced tomatoes; do not stir. Place the pressure lid onto the pot and make sure the valve is set to **Seal**. Press **Pressure** and set to **HI**. Set the timer to **4 minutes**, then press **Start**.

When the time is up, release the pressure by turning the valve to **Vent**. Carefully open the lid and gently stir in 1 cup (121 g) of the cheese. Sprinkle the top with the remaining cheese, close the lid and let it sit for **5 minutes** to allow the cheese to melt.

BOOYAH (HEARTY STEW WITH CHICKEN, BEEF & PORK)

SERVES 8

Functions Used
Sear/Saute, Pressure Cook

1 tbsp (15 ml) extra-virgin olive oil

1 lb (454 g) bone-in chicken thighs

1 lb (454 g) bone-in beef short ribs

1 lb (454 g) pork shoulder, cut into 1-inch (2.5-cm) pieces

1 yellow onion, chopped

1 celery rib, chopped

2 large carrots, chopped

5 cups (1 L) low-sodium chicken broth

2 cloves garlic

2 bay leaves

1 (14.5-oz [411-g]) can fire-roasted diced tomatoes, with liquid

1 lb (454 g) red potatoes, cut into bite-sized pieces

½ cup (75 g) frozen peas

2 cups (140 g) shredded green cabbage

1 tsp coarse salt

½ tsp freshly ground black pepper

1 tsp freshly squeezed lemon juice (more or less to your tastes, but don't skip it)

I grew up near Green Bay, Wisconsin, and Booyah was always a big event in the summertime. Neighbors gather together and cook it in one big pot, sometimes taking days to prepare it! I've scaled down this delicious, hearty stew so you can enjoy it in your Foodi. But I still encourage you to share it with your neighbors—they'll love you for it!

Press **Sear/Saute** and set the heat to **Medium**. Allow the Foodi to preheat for **5 minutes**.

Add the oil to the pot and when it's shimmering, add the chicken thighs, skin-side down. Cook until browned, about **5 minutes**, then flip and brown the opposite side. Remove the chicken and set aside, then repeat the process with the ribs and then the pork, browning them on all sides. Set all the meat aside.

Add the onion, celery and carrots, and cook for about **5 minutes**, stirring occasionally. Add the meat back to the pot, then add the broth, garlic, bay leaves, tomatoes and potatoes. Place the pressure lid onto the pot and make sure the valve is set to **Seal**. Press **Pressure** and set to **HI**. Set the timer to **30 minutes**, then press **Start**.

When the time is up, carefully release the pressure by turning the valve to **Vent**. Remove the pressure lid and remove the meat. The meat will just fall away from the bones; you can either pull it into bite-sized pieces or cut them, whatever is easier for you, then discard the bones. Remove the garlic and bay leaves from the pot.

Stir in the meat, peas and cabbage. Close the crisping lid and allow the stew to sit for **10 minutes**, until the peas and cabbage are soft. Add the salt, pepper and lemon juice before serving.

WILD MUSHROOM & BRIE SOUP

SERVES 4 TO 6

Functions Used
Air Crisp, Sear/Saute, Pressure Cook

Talk about decadence! This creamy, earthy soup is the epitome of indulgence. And it's so easy to make. I serve this soup at every Christmas dinner and everyone always raves about it. The Parmesan pepper croutons add the perfect texture contrast to the velvety soup.

For the Croutons
½ day-old French baguette, cut into bite-sized cubes

2 tbsp (30 ml) extra-virgin olive oil

½ tsp coarse salt

1–2 tsp (2–4 g) freshly ground black pepper

¼ cup (25 g) finely grated Parmesan cheese

For the Soup
2 tbsp (30 ml) ghee or canola oil

½ lb (227 g) crimini mushrooms, sliced

½ lb (227 g) button mushrooms, sliced

½ lb (227 g) shiitake mushrooms, stems removed, sliced

3 leeks, cleaned and sliced (white and light green parts only)

2 cloves garlic, minced

2 tbsp (16 g) flour

4 cups (946 ml) reduced sodium chicken broth

1 cup (237 ml) heavy cream

½ lb (227 g) brie, rind removed and cut into 10 small pieces

3 tbsp (45 ml) sherry

½ tsp coarse salt, more to taste

Make the croutons by placing the bread cubes in a medium-sized mixing bowl. Drizzle the olive oil over the bread cubes, then sprinkle with the salt and pepper. Toss well with your hands. Grate the Parmesan cheese over the top and toss gently.

Place the Cook & Crisp basket in the pot then place the croutons in the basket. Press **Air Crisp**, set the temperature to **390°F (199°C)** and the timer to **6 minutes**. When the time is up, open the lid, shake the basket and check the croutons to see if they're browned and crispy to your liking. Cook **1 to 2 minutes** more if desired, then remove them from the basket and spread them out on aluminum foil or waxed paper to cool.

To make the soup, press **Sear/Saute** and set the heat to **HI**. Allow the Foodi to preheat for **5 minutes**. Add the ghee and once it's melted and hot, add the mushrooms. Cook until the mushrooms are nicely browned. Mushrooms will release their liquid first; once the liquid evaporates, the mushrooms will begin to brown. Reduce the heat to **Medium**. Add the leeks and cook for **3 to 4 minutes**, stirring occasionally. Add the garlic and cook for **1 minute**, stirring frequently.

Sprinkle the mushroom mixture with the flour. Cook for **1 minute**, stirring frequently. Slowly whisk in the chicken broth. Place the pressure lid onto the pot and make sure the valve is set to **Seal**. Press **Pressure** and set to **HI**. Set the timer to **10 minutes**, then press **Start**.

When the time is up, carefully release the remaining pressure by turning the valve to **Vent**. When all the pressure is released, remove the lid.

Using an immersion blender, or a regular blender in batches, blend the soup until it's smooth. Stir in the cream, brie and sherry. Continue stirring until the brie has melted and is fully incorporated. Stir in the salt. Pour the soup into serving bowls and top with the Parmesan pepper croutons.

EXTRA-BEEFY CHILI

SERVES 8 TO 10

Functions Used
Sear/Saute, Pressure Cook

1 tbsp (15 ml) extra-virgin olive oil

1 large sweet onion, chopped

2 medium poblano peppers, chopped

4 lbs (1.8 kg) ground beef

3 tbsp (24 g) chili powder

1 tsp chipotle chili powder

1 tsp ancho chili powder

1½ tsp (3 g) ground cumin

½ cup (119 ml) water

3 (14-oz [411-g]) cans fire-roasted diced tomatoes, with liquid

2 (14-oz [411-g]) cans tomato sauce

1 tsp coarse salt

¼ tsp freshly ground black pepper

If you're not a bean lover, or if you just happen to love beef, then this hearty chili is for you! Made with a whopping 4 pounds (1.8 kg) of beef, this one will satisfy even the hungriest members of the family. Serve with a loaf of crusty bread or a side of garlic bread for dipping.

Press **Sear/Saute** and set the heat to **Medium**. Allow the Foodi to preheat for **5 minutes**.

Add the oil to the pot and when it's shimmering, add the onion and poblano peppers. Cook for about **5 minutes**, stirring frequently. Add the ground beef and cook it until almost no pink remains, **8 to 10 minutes**. Drain off the fat.

Add the chili powder, chipotle chili powder, ancho chili powder and cumin. Cook for **1 minute**, stirring frequently. Add the water to the pot, then the diced tomatoes, then the tomato sauce; do not stir. Place the pressure lid onto the pot and make sure the valve is set to **Seal**. Press **Pressure** and set to **HI**. Set the timer to **30 minutes**, then press **Start**.

When the time is up, carefully release the pressure by turning the valve to **Vent**. Remove the lid, then stir in the salt and pepper.

CHICKEN & SAUSAGE JAMBALAYA

SERVES 4

Functions Used
Sear/Saute, Pressure Cook

2 tbsp (30 ml) extra-virgin olive oil

1 (12-oz [340-g]) package andouille sausage, cut into bite-sized pieces

½ lb (227 g) boneless, skinless chicken breasts, cut into small bite-sized pieces

1 green bell pepper, seeded and chopped

1 yellow onion, chopped

3 celery ribs, chopped

3 cloves garlic, minced

2 tsp (10 g) Cajun seasoning

1 tsp dried basil

2 cups (473 ml) low-sodium chicken broth

1½ cups (316 g) long-grain white rice

1 (14.5-oz [411-g]) can fire-roasted diced tomatoes, with liquid

½ tsp coarse salt

2 green onions or 2 tbsp (5 g) fresh parsley, chopped (optional)

If you're looking for a hearty meal with loads of flavor, this jambalaya recipe is it! The Foodi cooks it all in one pot for you, and it's so good that everyone will be fighting over the leftovers.

Press **Sear/Saute** and set the heat to **Medium**. Allow the Foodi to preheat for **5 minutes**.

Add the oil to the pot and when it's shimmering, add the sausage. Cook for **3 to 4 minutes**, stirring occasionally, until it's browned on both sides. Remove the sausage with a slotted spoon.

Add the chicken and cook just until it's starting to brown, about **3 minutes**. Remove the chicken.

Add the bell pepper, onion, celery, garlic, Cajun seasoning and basil. Stir well to scrape up any browned bits from the bottom of the pot or your Foodi may not come to pressure later. Cook for about **2 minutes**. If there are still browned bits on the bottom of the pot after **2 minutes**, you can pour in a small amount of the chicken broth to make them easier to remove.

Without stirring, add the broth, rice, tomatoes, salt and reserved sausage and chicken to the pot. Place the pressure lid onto the pot and make sure the valve is set to **Seal**. Press **Pressure** and set to **HI**. Set the timer to **5 minutes**, then press **Start**.

When the time is up, allow the pressure to release naturally for **5 minutes**, then carefully release the remaining pressure by turning the valve to **Vent**. Carefully open the lid, fluff the rice with a fork and transfer to a serving dish. Top with the chopped green onions or parsley (if desired).

COTTAGE PIE WITH PARMESAN POTATOES

SERVES 6 TO 8

Functions Used
Pressure Cook, Sear/Saute, Bake/Roast

When it's hot outside and you're craving a hearty meal but don't want to turn on your oven, try this cottage pie. It's layered with flavor and the Parmesan potatoes really put it over the top!

For the Potatoes
3 lbs (1.4 kg) red potatoes, cut into quarters or sixths

1 cup (237 ml) chicken broth

¼ cup (60 g) butter, softened

1½ cups (355 ml) milk, room temperature

1 tsp coarse salt

For the Filling
½ lb (227 g) green beans

2 lbs (907 g) ground beef

1 medium onion, chopped

1 carrot, peeled and diced

1 lb (454 g) sliced mushrooms

3 cloves garlic, minced

1 tsp dried thyme

3 tbsp (46 g) tomato paste

3 tbsp (23 g) flour

½ cup (118 ml) red wine

3 cups (710 ml) beef stock or broth

2 tbsp (31 g) Worcestershire sauce

1 tsp coarse salt

¼ tsp freshly ground black pepper

2 tbsp (30 g) butter, melted

¼–½ cup (25–50 g) grated Parmesan cheese

Place the potatoes and chicken broth in the pot. Place the pressure lid onto the pot and make sure the valve is set to **Seal**. Press **Pressure** and set to **HI**. Set the timer to **8 minutes**, then press **Start**.

When the time is up, carefully release the pressure by turning the valve to **Vent**, then remove the lid once all the pressure is released. Add the butter, milk and salt. Mash with a potato masher until smooth, adding more milk if necessary. Set the potatoes aside while you make the filling and wipe out the inside of the pot.

To make the filling, press **Sear/Saute** and set the heat to **Medium**. Allow the Foodi to preheat for **5 minutes**. Meanwhile, trim the green beans and cut them into ½-inch (1-cm) pieces. Set aside. When the Foodi has preheated, put the ground beef in the pot and cook, stirring occasionally, until no pink remains, **6 to 7 minutes**. Remove the beef with a slotted spoon and set aside. Drain all but 1 tablespoon (15 ml) of fat from the pot.

Add the onion, carrot, mushrooms and green beans to the pot, cooking for **4 to 5 minutes** or until the onion is soft. Add the garlic and thyme and cook for **1 to 2 minutes**, stirring frequently. Stir in the tomato paste. Sprinkle in the flour and stir well for **1 minute**. Add the red wine and stir to combine. Whisk in the beef stock and Worcestershire until it's smooth. Season well with salt and pepper.

Carefully spread the mashed potatoes over the filling, taking care to cover the filling completely. Drizzle the potatoes with the melted butter, then sprinkle the top with Parmesan.

Close the crisping lid. Press **Bake/Roast** and set the temperature to **350°F (177°C)** and the timer to **30 minutes**. Press **Start**. After it's done, allow the cottage pie to rest for **10 minutes** before serving.

DORITOS® TACO CASSEROLE WITH BLACK BEANS & CORN

SERVES 4

Functions Used
Sear/Saute, Bake/Roast

1 lb (454 g) ground beef

½ large onion, chopped

1 (1-oz [28-g]) packet taco seasoning

½ cup (118 ml) water

1 cup (246 g) tomatillo salsa, plus more for serving

½ cup (110 g) sour cream, plus more for serving

1 (15-oz [425-g]) can black beans, rinsed and drained

1 (14.5-oz [411-g]) can corn, drained

4 cups (230 g) crushed Doritos

2 cups (241 g) shredded Mexican-blend cheese

Optional Toppings
Sour cream

Avocado

Chopped cilantro

Cherry tomatoes, halved

When I make this casserole, I say that I'm making it because the kids love it. But secretly, it's one of my favorite meal repeats because it's so easy and delicious! The Doritos add a lot of flavor and texture, and the kids get to think that I'm doing it just for them.

Press **Sear/Saute** and set the heat to **Medium**. Allow the Foodi to preheat for **5 minutes**. Add the ground beef and onion to the pot. Cook for about **5 minutes**, stirring occasionally until no pink remains in the beef.

Add the taco seasoning and water, stirring well. Cook for about **2 minutes** or until it's slightly thickened. Add the salsa and sour cream; stir well. Add the black beans and corn; stir well and press **Stop** to turn off the heat. Put the mixture in a medium-sized bowl.

Place half of the crushed Doritos in the bottom of the pot, then put half the taco mixture on top, followed by 1 cup (121 g) of the cheese. Repeat with remaining Doritos and taco mixture, then end with the remaining cheese.

Press **Bake/Roast**, then set the temperature to **375°F (191°C)** and the timer to **15 minutes**. Press **Start**. Bake until it's bubbling and the cheese is melted. Top with your desired toppings. Serve with extra salsa and sour cream on the side.

SWEET & SMOKY TAMALE PIE

SERVES 6

Functions Used
Sear/Saute, Bake/Roast

2 tsp (10 ml) extra-virgin olive oil

1 lb (454 g) ground beef

1 small yellow onion, chopped

1 poblano pepper, chopped

2 cloves garlic, minced

1½ tsp (3 g) ground cumin

½ tsp ancho chile powder

1 (15-oz [425-g]) can black beans, rinsed and drained

1 cup (136 g) frozen corn

1 cup (200 g) diced tomatoes

2 chipotle chiles, minced (from a can of chipotle chiles in adobo sauce)

1 (8.5-oz [240-g]) package cornbread mix (such as Jiffy)

Optional Toppings
Sour cream

Chopped cilantro

Diced tomatoes

Shredded cheese

This recipe is where the Foodi really shines. Saute your ingredients for the filling of this tamale pie, then bake the cornbread topping, all in the same pot! You'll love the smoky heat from the chipotle peppers and the perfectly cooked cornbread without the extra dishes to wash.

Press **Sear/Saute** and set the temperature to **Medium**. Add the oil to the pot and when it's shimmering, add the ground beef, onion, poblano pepper and garlic. Cook the ground beef mixture until there's no pink remaining, **6 to 8 minutes**. Carefully remove the pot and drain off any fat.

Return the pot to the Foodi and add the cumin, chile powder, black beans, corn, diced tomatoes and chipotle chiles. Press **Sear/Saute** and set the temperature to **LO**, then set the timer to **10 minutes**. Stir the mixture occasionally while it simmers.

Meanwhile, make the cornbread batter according to the package directions. When the time is up, place heaping spoonfuls of the batter on top of the ground beef mixture, covering as much of the filling as possible using equal spoonfuls of batter. Close the crisping lid. Press **Bake/Roast** and set the timer to **15 minutes**.

When the time is up, open the crisping lid and make sure the cornbread is cooked through (a toothpick or tester inserted in the middle should come out free of wet batter), adding more time if necessary. Scoop into bowls and serve with desired toppings.

TARRAGON CHICKEN & POTATOES

SERVES 4

Functions Used
Sear/Saute, Pressure Cook

2 tbsp (30 ml) extra-virgin olive oil

½ lb (227 g) crimini mushrooms, sliced

4 boneless, skinless chicken breasts or thighs, about 1 lb (454 g), cut into bite-size pieces

¼ cup (59 ml) dry white wine

1 tbsp (8 g) flour

1 cup (237 ml) chicken broth or stock

½ lb (227 g) baby red potatoes, cut in half or into quarters depending on their size

½ cup (110 g) sour cream

2 tsp (10 g) Dijon mustard

2 tbsp (5 g) fresh tarragon, finely chopped , plus more for garnish

½ tsp coarse salt

¼ tsp freshly ground black pepper

Tarragon is one of my favorite herbs, and it's not used enough in cooking, in my opinion. This light yet hearty meal is what I cook when I want something a little different but that will still please the entire family.

Press **Sear/Saute** and set the heat to **Medium**. Allow the Foodi to preheat for **5 minutes**.

Add the oil to the pot and when it's shimmering, add the mushrooms. Cook for about **5 minutes**, stirring occasionally until they're starting to brown.

Add the chicken and cook just until it's starting to brown, about **3 minutes**. Add the wine and cook for about **2 minutes**, until it's reduced by about half. Sprinkle the flour into the pot and cook for about **1 minute**, stirring frequently. Whisk in the chicken broth until it's smooth. Add the potatoes to the pot. Place the pressure lid onto the pot and make sure the valve is set to **Seal**. Press **Pressure** and set to **HI**. Set the timer to **20 minutes**, then press **Start**.

When the time is up, allow the pressure to release naturally for **5 minutes**, then carefully release the remaining pressure by turning the valve to **Vent**. Open the lid and stir in the sour cream, mustard and tarragon. Season with the salt and pepper and garnish with extra chopped tarragon if you'd like.

CREAMY BAKED ZITI WITH ITALIAN SAUSAGE

SERVES 6 TO 8

Functions Used
Sear/Saute, Bake/Roast, Broil (optional, see note)

1 lb (454 g) ziti pasta

1 tbsp (15 ml) extra-virgin olive oil

1 medium sweet onion, chopped

1 lb (454 g) lean ground beef

1 lb (454 g) ground Italian sausage

3 cloves garlic, minced

2 jars spaghetti sauce, about 52 oz (1.5 kg) total

1 (14.5-oz [411-g]) can fire-roasted diced tomatoes, with liquid

1 (8-oz [227-g]) package cream cheese, softened

1 (16-oz [454-g]) container whole milk ricotta cheese

½ cup (110 g) sour cream

½ cup (50 g) grated Parmesan cheese

1 tsp coarse salt

¼ tsp freshly ground black pepper

3 cups (362 g) shredded mozzarella cheese

¼ cup (10 g) chopped parsley

The secret to this super creamy baked pasta is cream cheese. It adds so much to this pasta, plus you can brown the top right in your Ninja Foodi. The beef, sausage, tomatoes and creamy cheeses combine for a flavor and texture that can't be beat.

On the stovetop, cook the pasta according to the package directions until just al dente. Be careful not to cook the pasta all the way to tender, as it will continue cooking as it's baked with the sauce.

Meanwhile, press **Sear/Saute** and set the heat to **Medium**. Allow the Foodi to preheat for **5 minutes**.

Add the oil to the Foodi and when it's shimmering, add the onion. Cook for **2 minutes**, stirring occasionally. Add the ground beef and sausage; cook until no pink remains, about **7 to 8 minutes**. Add the garlic and cook for **1 minute**, stirring frequently. Stir in the spaghetti sauce and tomatoes.

In a medium-sized mixing bowl, mix together cream cheese, ricotta and sour cream just until combined and smooth. Stir in the Parmesan, salt and pepper.

Add the al dente pasta to the Foodi pot and stir well to combine. Top with the ricotta mixture, spreading it out to cover (it's okay if it mixes in a little with the pasta). Top it all with the mozzarella. Close the crisping lid. Press **Bake/Roast** and set the temperature to **350°F (177°C)** and the timer to **30 minutes**. Press **Start**.

When the time is up, open the lid and sprinkle with chopped parsley. Allow to sit for **10 minutes** before serving.

Note: If you prefer the cheese browned, after the dish is done baking you may close the crisping lid, press **Broil** and set the timer to **2 minutes**, checking after **1 minute** to see if it's browned to your liking.

CHICKEN ALFREDO PASTA BAKE

SERVES 4

Functions Used
Sear/Saute, Bake/Roast

Creamy alfredo sauce combined with ricotta cheese and tender chicken makes for a unique, indulgent meal that comes together quickly in your Foodi. Kids will love this one!

For the Alfredo Sauce
¾ cup (180 g) butter

1½ cups (355 ml) heavy cream

3 cups (300 g) finely grated Parmesan

1 cup (240 g) sour cream (see note)

½ tsp coarse salt

¼ tsp freshly ground black pepper

For the Baked Pasta
1 lb (454 g) penne pasta

2 large eggs

1 (16-oz [454-g]) container ricotta cheese (see note)

¼ cup (25 g) grated Parmesan cheese

3 cups (420 g) cooked, shredded chicken

2 cups (241 g) shredded mozzarella cheese

1 tbsp (3 g) chopped parsley

Note: Try a lightened-up version by swapping out full-fat sour cream and ricotta for low-fat.

To make the Alfredo sauce, press **Sear/Saute** and set the heat to **Medium**. Allow the Foodi to preheat for **5 minutes**. Place the butter and heavy cream into the pot and heat it until it's hot and steaming; do not boil. Turn off the heat, then slowly stir in the Parmesan until it's completely smooth. Stir in the sour cream. Season to taste with the salt and pepper, adding more if necessary. Keep warm until the pasta is done cooking.

Meanwhile, make the penne pasta in a separate pot on the stovetop. Cook the pasta according to the package directions. When it's ready, drain and immediately pour the cooked pasta into the sauce in the Foodi, gently tossing to make sure it's entirely coated with the sauce.

Lightly beat the eggs in a small bowl. Stir in the ricotta and Parmesan, mixing it thoroughly. Stir in the shredded chicken and set aside.

Remove half of the pasta from the pot. Spoon the ricotta mixture over the pasta left in the pot, then top with the reserved pasta. Sprinkle the top of the pasta with the mozzarella.

Close the crisping lid. Press **Bake/Roast** and set the temperature to **350°F (177°C)** and the timer to **25 minutes**. Press **Start**. When the time is up, sprinkle with the chopped parsley.

PRACTICALLY NO-PREP MEALS

The best thing about the Foodi is that it does all the heavy lifting for you: It pressure cooks your ingredients until they're tender and flavorful, it crisps up chicken and the tops of casseroles or lasagna, and you can even top your meals with biscuits and bake them right in the pot! The only thing it can't do is chop and slice your ingredients beforehand, so I created some simple, flavorful recipes for those nights you need to skip the prep but still have a warm, comforting meal on the table at the end of the day. "Roast" a whole chicken with just a few spices, make an entire pot pie without chopping anything more than an onion or serve an entire meal with potatoes and carrots on the side without ever having picked up a knife. These recipes are my busy night go-to's that my family loves, and I know yours will too!

My Three Favorites

Portobello BBQ "Sandwiches" (page 57)

Bacon & Blue Cheese Potato Soup (page 58)

Parmesan Pork Chops & Brussels Sprouts (page 65)

SMOKY ROTISSERIE-STYLE WHOLE CHICKEN

SERVES 4

Functions Used
Pressure Cook, Air Crisp

Being able to cook an entire chicken that actually gets crispy, browned skin is one of my favorite features of the Ninja Foodi! The chicken is juicy and fall-off-the-bone tender from being pressure cooked, then the crisping lid turns it golden brown as if you'd cooked it in the oven. The result is just like rotisserie chicken, except cheaper and without any mystery ingredients. I created a bold spice rub for this recipe, but it's easy to change up with different seasonings.

1 tsp paprika

1 tsp smoked paprika

1 tsp garlic powder

1 tsp onion powder

1 tsp dried thyme

1 tsp coarse salt

½ tsp coarsely ground black pepper

½ cup (118 ml) water

1 whole chicken, 4–5 lbs (1.8–2.3 kg) (see notes)

Cooking spray

In a small bowl, mix together the paprika, smoked paprika, garlic powder, onion powder, thyme, salt and pepper. Rub the mixture all over the outside of the chicken. Pour the water into the pot.

Place the chicken in the Cook & Crisp basket, then place the basket inside the pot. Put the pressure lid on and turn it to make sure it's on securely. Make sure the valve is set to **Seal**, then select **Pressure** and set to **HI**. Set the timer to **22 minutes**, then press **Start**.

When the time is up, allow the pressure to release naturally for **5 minutes**, then release any remaining pressure by moving the pressure release valve to **Vent**. Carefully remove the lid once all the pressure has been released.

Spray the chicken with the cooking spray, then close the crisping lid. Set the temperature to **400°F (204°C)** and set the timer to **8 minutes**. Select **Air Crisp** then **Start** to begin.

When the time is up, remove the Cook & Crisp basket from the Foodi, then remove the chicken and place it on a cutting board. Let the chicken rest for **5 minutes**, then carve it up and serve.

Notes: If you prefer even crispier chicken, simply close the crisping lid again after the **8 minutes** are up and add a few more minutes to the timer. If your chicken is on the smaller side (3 lbs [1.4 kg]), decrease the pressure-cooking time to **20 minutes**.

ALTERNATE SEASONING IDEAS

Lemon-Pepper: ¼ cup (40 g) store-bought lemon-pepper seasoning (or 2 tbsp [19 g] lemon zest, 1 tbsp [7 g] freshly ground black pepper and ½ tsp coarse salt)
Italian: 3 tsp (2 g) Italian seasoning, 2 tsp (6 g) lemon zest, 1 tsp coarse salt and ¼ tsp freshly ground black pepper
Mexican: 2 tbsp (28 g) brown sugar, 1½ tbsp (11 g) chipotle chili powder and 1 tbsp (7 g) smoked paprika

FALL-OFF-THE-BONE FOODI RIBS

SERVES 4

Functions Used
Pressure Cook, Air Crisp

Once you make ribs in your Ninja Foodi, you'll never spend hours cooking them low and slow again! These St. Louis–style ribs get fall-off-the-bone tender from being pressure cooked, then the barbecue sauce gets baked into the meat using the crisping lid. A smoky, peppery spice rub cooks flavor into the meat to really make the flavors sing! They're just as good as any ribs I've made in the oven or on the grill. This recipe was originally published in my first cookbook and turned out to be so popular that I'm sharing it here, too, with a few slight changes for even tastier ribs!

3 tbsp (42 g) brown sugar

1 tbsp (15 g) coarse salt

1½ tbsp (12 g) crushed black peppercorns

1½ tbsp (9 g) smoked paprika

2 tsp (4 g) garlic powder

3 lbs (1.3 kg) St. Louis–style ribs, cut into thirds

½ cup (118 ml) water

1 cup (246 g) barbecue sauce

To make the spice rub, combine the brown sugar, salt, crushed peppercorns, smoked paprika and garlic powder in a small bowl. Place the ribs on a cutting board, then rub the ribs all over with the spice rub mixture.

Pour the water into the pot. Place the Cook & Crisp basket inside the pot, then set the ribs inside the basket, standing them up along the outside. Put the pressure lid on and turn it to make sure it's on securely. Make sure the valve is set to **Seal**, then select **Pressure** and make sure it's set to **HI**. Set the timer to **20 minutes**, then press **Start**.

When the time is up, release the pressure by moving the pressure release valve to **Vent**. Carefully remove the lid once all the pressure has been released.

Close the crisping lid, press **Air Crisp**, set the temperature to **400°F (204°C)**, then set the timer to **15 minutes**. Select **Start** to begin. After **10 minutes**, open the crisping lid and brush the ribs all over with the barbecue sauce. You can do this with the ribs still in the pot by gently pulling them to the side and brushing the sauce on each rib. Close the lid and allow the ribs to keep cooking.

When the time is up, remove the Cook & Crisp basket from the Foodi, then remove the ribs and place them on a cutting board. Cut the ribs into pieces (about two ribs each) before serving.

PULLED PORK TACOS

SERVES 6 TO 8

Functions Used
Sear/Saute, Pressure Cook

For the Spice Rub
3 tbsp (24 g) chili powder

2 tbsp (16 g) chipotle chili powder

1 tbsp (6 g) ground cumin

1 tsp cayenne pepper

1½ tsp (3 g) onion powder

1½ tsp (3 g) garlic powder

1 tsp dried oregano

1½ tbsp (17 g) light brown sugar

1 tbsp (15 g) coarse salt

For the Pork
1 (5-lb [2.3-kg]) pork shoulder, cut into 4 equal pieces

1 tbsp (15 ml) extra-virgin olive oil

½ cup (118 ml) chicken broth or water

For Serving
12 corn tortillas

1 (16-oz [453-g]) jar salsa verde

½ cup (10 g) chopped cilantro

1 white onion, chopped

1 cup (121 g) crumbled queso fresco cheese

When you want to feed a crowd, reach for these pulled pork tacos. The flavor of the pork is amazing, and it gets incredibly tender in the Ninja Foodi! You can freeze any leftover pork so you can make these tacos anytime.

For the spice rub, mix the chili powder, chipotle chili powder, cumin, cayenne pepper, onion powder, garlic powder, dried oregano, brown sugar and salt in a small bowl. Then massage the mixture all over the pork shoulder.

Press **Sear/Saute** and set the heat to **Medium**. Allow the Foodi to preheat for **5 minutes**.

Add the oil to the pot and when it's shimmering, sear the pork on all sides until it's browned, then remove and set aside.

Add the chicken broth to the pot. Scrape up all the browned bits on the bottom of the pot. Place the pork roast back in the pot, setting it into the broth. Place the pressure lid onto the pot and make sure the valve is set to **Seal**. Press **Pressure** and set to **HI**. Set the timer to **90 minutes**, then press Start.

When the time is up, release the pressure manually by carefully turning the valve to **Vent**. When all of the pressure is released, open the lid and remove the roast. Place it on a cutting board, then shred the meat using two forks.

To serve, place some of the meat on a corn tortilla, then top with the salsa verde, chopped cilantro, chopped white onion and crumbled queso fresco.

CRISPY HASH BROWNS & EGGS

SERVES 2 TO 3

Functions Used
Air Crisp

Cooking spray

2 cups (360 g) frozen hash browns

2 tbsp (30 g) unsalted butter, cut into 8 small squares

2–4 large eggs

½ tsp coarse salt

¼ tsp freshly ground black pepper

This is a frequent breakfast at our house because it's so simple and tastes so good. I keep frozen hash browns in my freezer at all times so I can make it on a moment's notice. It's so simple to make in the Ninja Foodi that my kids make it for themselves!

Spray the bottom of the pot with cooking spray. Add the hash browns, then spray the top of the hash browns with more cooking spray and dot with the butter squares. Press **Air Crisp**, set the temperature to **390°F (199°C)** and the timer to **7 minutes**.

When the time is up, shake the hash browns in the pot. Using a spoon, press into the hash browns to create small, round indentations (this will help keep the eggs in place). Crack an egg into each indentation, then season the eggs and hash browns with the salt and pepper. Set the temperature to **325°F (163°C)** (still using the **Air Crisp** function), close the lid and set the timer to **10 minutes**. Cook until the eggs are done to your liking (**10 minutes** will result in medium-cooked eggs).

PORTOBELLO BBQ "SANDWICHES"

SERVES 4

Functions Used
Bake/Roast

For the Coleslaw

½ cup (110 g) mayonnaise

1 tbsp (12 g) sugar

1 tbsp (15 ml) apple cider vinegar

1 tsp celery seeds

2 tsp (10 g) Dijon mustard

1 (8-oz [227-g]) bag coleslaw mix

½ tsp coarse salt

¼ tsp freshly ground black pepper

For the Mushrooms

4 portobello mushroom caps, stems removed and the gills scraped off

1 tbsp (15 ml) extra-virgin olive oil

For the Chicken

2 cups (280 g) cooked, shredded rotisserie chicken, room temperature

¾ cup (91 g) shredded mozzarella cheese, divided

½ tsp coarse salt

½ cup (123 g) barbecue sauce

I love a hearty barbecue sandwich with a creamy, crunchy coleslaw on top. This recipe omits the bun but still delivers the flavorful, filling "sandwich" that I want. It's low-carb, healthy and oh-so-delicious!

To make the coleslaw, mix together the mayonnaise, sugar, vinegar, celery seeds and mustard in a medium-sized bowl. Gently fold in the coleslaw mix, salt and pepper until the coleslaw mix is thoroughly coated. Cover and refrigerate until ready to serve.

To make the mushrooms, brush the mushrooms with the olive oil on both sides and place in the pot. Press **Bake/Roast** and set the temperature to **350°F (177°C)** and the timer to **12 minutes**. Press **Start**. When the time is up, remove the mushrooms from the pot, drain off all the liquid and pat them dry.

Meanwhile, mix the chicken, ½ cup (60 g) of the mozzarella, the salt and the barbecue sauce in a bowl. Fill the mushrooms evenly with the chicken filling, then top with the remaining mozzarella; add more if desired.

Place the mushrooms back into the pot and bake for about **15 minutes**, or until the cheese is melted and the filling is heated through. Place the mushrooms on a serving platter, then top each mushroom with the coleslaw.

BACON & BLUE CHEESE POTATO SOUP

SERVES 6 TO 8

Functions Used
Sear/Saute, Pressure Cook

If you love a hot creamy potato soup, then this is one you'll definitely want to try. There's no peeling your potatoes and no separate boiling and draining them. The subtle blue cheese flavor adds a richness that makes a surprisingly upscale soup from the ubiquitous potato. Serve this with a salad and you'll have a well-rounded meal on the table in under an hour.

½ lb (227 g) bacon, cut crosswise into 1-inch (2.5-cm) pieces

½ medium onion, chopped

2 cloves garlic, minced

3 tbsp (23 g) flour

1 (32-oz [909-ml]) container low-sodium chicken broth

3 lbs (1.4 kg) red potatoes, quartered

1 cup (121 g) crumbled blue cheese

2 cups (474 ml) whole milk

1 tsp coarse salt

¼ tsp freshly ground black pepper

2 tbsp (5 g) chopped chives

Press **Sear/Saute** and set the heat to **Medium**. Allow the Foodi to preheat for **5 minutes**. Cook the bacon pieces until they are browned and crispy, then remove them with a slotted spoon and place on paper towels to drain excess grease.

Add the onion to the drippings in the pot and cook until the onion is soft, about **5 minutes**, stirring frequently. Add the garlic and cook for **1 minute**, stirring frequently. Add the flour and cook for **1 minute**, stirring constantly. Add the chicken broth, taking care to scrape any brown bits from the bottom of the pot. Add the potatoes to the pot. Place the pressure lid onto the pot and make sure the valve is set to **Seal**. Press **Pressure** and set to **HI**. Set the timer to **20 minutes**, then press **Start**.

When the time is up, allow the pressure to release naturally for **5 minutes**, then carefully release the remaining pressure by turning the valve to **Vent**. Using a potato masher or something similar, crush the potatoes to thicken the soup, leaving some chunks.

Add the blue cheese and the milk, stirring until the cheese is completely melted and incorporated. Season with the salt and pepper. Mix the bacon into the soup or use it to top each bowl (or a little of both). Sprinkle each bowl with some of the chopped chives.

GARLIC BREAD HAM & SWISS SANDWICHES

SERVES 6

Functions Used
Bake/Roast

If you read that title and thought these are typical sandwiches, you'd be wrong! They're hot and cheesy, and the butter mixture that bakes into the bread makes them sandwiches you won't soon forget. Using your Foodi to bake these means your oven won't heat up your house! Make these for an easy weeknight meal or serve them for your next football party.

6 French rolls

½ lb (227 g) sliced ham

¼ red onion, sliced

1 jalapeño pepper, thinly sliced (optional)

6 slices Swiss cheese

½ cup (120 g) butter

4 cloves garlic, minced

¼ cup (25 g) grated Parmesan cheese

¼ cup (15 g) chopped parsley

Cut off the top third from the French rolls lengthwise. Hollow out the inside of each roll until there's just a shell left. Layer the ham inside each roll, followed by the red onion, jalapeño (if using) and Swiss cheese. Place the top of the bread back on to cover.

Make crosswise cuts into each roll, leaving just the very bottom of each one intact. Place the rolls onto individual sheets of aluminum foil that are large enough to wrap them in. Don't wrap them just yet.

In a small bowl, melt the butter in the microwave, then stir in the garlic, Parmesan and chopped parsley. Spoon the butter mixture evenly over the rolls, taking care to spread it out and ensure that some of the mixture seeps between the slices. Wrap up each roll tightly with aluminum foil and place in the pot (it's okay if the rolls overlap).

Close the crisping lid. Press **Bake/Roast** and set the temperature to **350°F (177°C)** and the timer to **30 minutes**. Press **Start**. Carefully remove the sandwich packets and unwrap the foil. Cut each sandwich into slices before serving.

CHICKEN TORTILLA SOUP

SERVES 6

Corn tortillas are used to thicken this flavorful soup without any high-calorie cream. It's a hearty meal that takes no time at all to make in your Foodi.

Functions Used
Sear/Saute, Pressure Cook

2 tsp (10 ml) extra-virgin olive oil

1 lb (454 g) boneless, skinless chicken breasts, cut into bite-sized pieces

½ white onion, chopped

2 cloves garlic, minced

1 tsp ground cumin

1 (14.5-oz [411-g]) can fire-roasted diced tomatoes

4 cups (946 ml) reduced-sodium chicken broth

1 (4-oz [113-g]) can diced green chiles

4 corn tortillas, torn into small pieces

½ tsp coarse salt

¼ cup (5 g) cilantro, chopped

Optional Toppings
Sour cream

Crushed tortilla chips

Chopped cilantro

Avocado

Lime wedges

Press **Sear/Saute** and set the heat to **Medium**. Allow the Foodi to preheat for **5 minutes**. Add the oil to the pot and when it's shimmering, add the chicken. Cook until the chicken is browned, about **5 minutes**. Remove the chicken with a slotted spoon.

Add the onion and cook until the onion is soft, **4 to 5 minutes**. Add the garlic and cumin and cook for **1 minute**, stirring frequently. Add the reserved chicken, tomatoes, broth, green chiles and tortillas to the pot. Stir well and scrape the bottom of the pot to remove any browned bits. Place the pressure lid onto the pot and make sure the valve is set to **Seal**. Press **Pressure** and set to **HI**. Set the timer to **20 minutes**, then press **Start**.

When the time is up, allow the pressure to release naturally. Carefully remove the pressure lid and stir the soup. Stir in the salt and the chopped cilantro. Ladle into bowls and serve with your desired toppings.

PARMESAN PORK CHOPS & BRUSSELS SPROUTS

SERVES 4

Functions Used
Air Crisp

2 tbsp (30 g) unsalted butter, melted

½ cup (50 g) grated Parmesan cheese

2 tsp (10 g) garlic salt

1 tsp onion powder

½ tsp freshly ground black pepper

4 bone-in pork chops, 1 inch (2.5 cm) thick, about 2 lbs (907 g)

1 lb (454 g) Brussels sprouts, trimmed and halved

½ tsp coarse salt

1 tbsp (15 ml) extra-virgin olive oil

If you've never air-fried pork chops before, you're in for a real treat! They turn out juicy on the inside with a nice crust on the outside, and the Brussels sprouts get perfectly charred at the same time.

Combine the melted butter, Parmesan, garlic salt, onion powder and black pepper in a small dish. Rub the mixture on all sides of the pork chops.

Toss the Brussels sprouts, salt and oil in a medium bowl. Place the Brussels sprouts in the pot, then place the pork chops on top. Press **Air Crisp**, set the temperature to **390°F (199°C)** and allow the Foodi to preheat for **5 minutes**.

When it's preheated, set the timer to **15 minutes** and press **Start**. When **8 minutes** is up, flip the pork chops and continue cooking until the pork is cooked through and the sprouts are cooked and crispy.

GARLIC-HERB TURKEY BREAST

SERVES 6 TO 8

Functions Used
Air Crisp

⅓ cup (80 g) unsalted butter, softened

2 cloves garlic, minced

1 tbsp (3 g) chopped fresh oregano

1 tbsp (3 g) chopped fresh rosemary

¼ tsp coarse salt

¼ tsp freshly ground black pepper

1 (4-lb [1.8-kg]) turkey breast (skin-on)

A tender, juicy turkey with crispy skin makes for an easy, delicious meal. I've made this turkey breast for a small holiday gathering, but it's also great to slice and use for sandwiches. The meat freezes well too!

Mix together the butter, garlic, oregano, rosemary, salt and pepper in a small bowl. Gently loosen the skin covering the turkey breast with your fingers, then rub all but 1 tablespoon (14 g) of the butter mixture all over the breast underneath the skin. Rub the remaining butter mixture onto the outside of the skin.

Press **Air Crisp**, set the temperature to **350°F (177°C)** and allow the Foodi to preheat for **5 minutes**. When it's preheated, set the timer to **15 minutes**, add the turkey to the pot, skin side down, and press **Start**.

When the time is up, flip the turkey breast so the skin is facing up, and reset the timer to **40 minutes**. Cook until the turkey breast is completely cooked through and the skin is browned and crispy.

CHICKEN, GREEN CHILE & POTATO PIE

SERVES 6

Functions Used
Bake/Roast

Savory casserole-style pies, like shepherd's pie, are one of my secret weapons for easy meals. This is one of my family's favorites for its creamy, flavorful filling paired with a flaky crust. When I've really been in a pinch, I've picked up sliced refrigerated potatoes (such as Simply Potatoes brand), which eliminates the only prep step! Everyone I've served it to loves it, and I know you will too.

5 eggs, divided

¾ cups (177 ml) heavy cream

½ cup (118 ml) whole milk

2 (4-oz [113-g]) cans diced green chiles

1 tsp coarse salt

½ tsp freshly ground black pepper

Cooking spray

2 russet potatoes, peeled and sliced very thin

3 cups (420 g) cooked, shredded chicken

2 cups (241 g) shredded Mexican-blend or Cheddar cheese

1 refrigerated pie crust

Separate one of the eggs, placing the yolk in a medium-sized mixing bowl and the white in a small dish; set aside the egg white. Add the remaining 4 eggs to the mixing bowl with the egg yolk. Beat the eggs until frothy, then whisk in the cream and milk. Add the green chiles, salt and pepper, then stir well.

Spray the Foodi pot with cooking spray. Arrange the potatoes in the bottom of the pot so they're slightly overlapping. Top the potatoes evenly with the chicken and cheese. Pour the egg mixture into the pot, pouring it evenly to ensure everything is covered.

Top the filling with the pie crust, then brush with the egg white. Cut a few slits in the crust to allow it to vent. Close the crisping lid. Press **Bake/Roast** and set the temperature to **350°F (177°C)** and the timer to **30 minutes**. Press **Start**. Once the pie has finished cooking, allow it to cool for **10 minutes** before serving.

AIR-FRIED DINNERS & SNACKS

The fact that the Foodi air-fries foods so well in addition to baking and pressure cooking is just incredible. Before I tried it, I was skeptical that it could do all of those things well. Yet everything I've thrown at it has come out crispy on the outside while maintaining a juicy inside. I don't know how Ninja does it, but I'm sure glad they figured it out! It's a rare day that I turn on my oven anymore, and I never do when it's hot out. And it's not just for breaded foods either; whole turkey breasts, fish, chicken and pork all turn out wonderfully! I've even included a recipe for air-fried rib-eyes, and they are so delicious and simple that you'll never make them any other way!

My Three Favorites

Fried Deviled Eggs (page 77)

Easy Chicken Taquitos (page 90)

Rib-Eyes with Compound Butter (page 100)

CRISPY PICKLE SPEARS

SERVES 4

Functions Used
Air Crisp

A local restaurant we frequent has the best fried pickles around. They have a subtle spice and they still have a slight crunch, and the outside is hot, crispy and flavorful. This is my ode to their pickles, and they're pretty darn close! Panko breadcrumbs make all the difference, and you can omit the cayenne if you prefer no spice at all.

1 (24-oz [709-ml]) jar dill pickle spears

¾ cup (94 g) all-purpose flour

½ tsp cayenne pepper (optional)

1 egg, beaten

1 cup (56 g) panko breadcrumbs

Cooking spray

⅓ cup (82 g) ranch dressing, for serving (optional)

Remove the pickles from the jar and dry them thoroughly on paper towels. Set out three shallow bowls. In the first bowl, place the flour and whisk in the cayenne pepper (if using). Place the egg into the second bowl, and the breadcrumbs into the third bowl. Dip each spear into the flour, then the egg, then the breadcrumbs.

Place the Cook & Crisp basket in the Foodi, set the temperature to **390°F (199°C)**, press **Air Crisp** and allow the Foodi to preheat for **5 minutes**. Place the breaded pickles into the basket in a single layer, just enough to fit (you'll do this in two batches). Spray the pickles with cooking spray. Set the timer to **15 minutes** and press **Start**.

Cook the pickles until they're browned and crispy, turning once halfway through the cooking time. Serve with ranch dressing for dipping, if desired.

BEER-BATTERED FISH TACOS

SERVES 3 TO 4

Functions Used
Air Crisp

Friday night fish fries are big in Wisconsin where I grew up, and I don't believe we ever missed one! So I know what makes a good fried fish: a light batter that doesn't overwhelm the tender, flaky fish. The combination of the delicate fish combined with the creamy sauce and crunchy cabbage is out of this world. If you love fish tacos, you must try this recipe! The fish is even great on its own, dipped into the sauce or with a traditional tartar sauce.

For the Sauce
½ cup (110 g) mayonnaise

½ cup (110 g) sour cream

Juice of 1 lime

½ tsp dried oregano

½ tsp ground cumin

1 tsp cayenne pepper

1 jalapeño, stem and seeds removed, then minced

½ cup (10 g) fresh cilantro, chopped

For the Batter
1 egg, beaten

1 cup (237 ml) Mexican beer

1 cup (125 g) flour

1 tsp baking powder

2 tbsp (19 g) cornstarch

½ tsp coarse salt

For the Fish
1 lb (454 g) white fish (such as tilapia or cod), cut into 6 pieces

½ tsp coarse salt

¼ tsp freshly ground black pepper

For Serving
6 corn tortillas

1 cup (70 g) shredded green cabbage

¼ cup (5 g) chopped fresh cilantro

For the sauce, mix together the mayonnaise, sour cream, lime juice, dried oregano, cumin, cayenne pepper, jalapeño and chopped cilantro in a medium bowl. Allow the sauce to sit at room temperature while you prepare the rest of the dish. Alternatively, you can make it ahead of time and store it in the refrigerator for up to 3 days.

Place the Cook & Crisp basket in the pot. Press **Air Crisp**, set the temperature to **375°F (191°C)** and allow the Foodi to preheat for **5 minutes**.

For the batter, in a shallow dish, whisk together the egg and beer. In another shallow dish, mix together the flour, baking powder, cornstarch and salt. Season the fish with the salt and pepper. Dip the fish into the egg mixture then immediately into the flour mixture. Once the Foodi is preheated, place the fish inside the basket in a single layer and set the timer to **15 minutes**.

When the time is up, remove the fish and divide it evenly among the tortillas. Top with some of the sauce and some green cabbage and chopped cilantro.

FRIED DEVILED EGGS

SERVES 6 TO 8

Functions Used
Pressure Cook, Air Crisp

1 dozen large eggs, plus 2 beaten eggs for dredging

⅓ cup (73 g) mayonnaise

¼ cup (55 g) sour cream

1 tsp Dijon mustard

½ tsp hot sauce

½ tsp coarse salt

½ cup (62 g) all-purpose flour

2 cups (112 g) panko breadcrumbs

Cooking spray

I could eat deviled eggs all day long, but when you add a crispy breading to the tender whites, it takes them to a whole new level. Air-frying is the easiest way to get that crunch you're looking for!

To hard-boil your eggs in the Foodi, pour 1 cup (237 ml) of water into the pot, then place the Cook & Crisp basket inside. Gently put the dozen eggs into the basket (no pun intended). Place the pressure lid onto the pot and make sure the valve is set to **Seal**. Press **Pressure** and set to **HI**. Set the timer to **7 minutes**, then press **Start**. Prepare an ice bath by filling a medium-sized bowl with ice then water.

When the time is up, carefully release the pressure by turning the valve to **Vent**. When all of the pressure is released, open the lid and place the eggs in the ice bath to cool.

When the eggs are completely cooled, peel them, slice them in half lengthwise and remove the yolks. In a medium bowl, mix together the yolks, mayonnaise, sour cream, mustard, hot sauce and salt until very smooth. Use a fork to vigorously break up the yolks if necessary. Set the mixture aside until you're ready to fill the egg whites.

Place the flour, 2 beaten eggs and breadcrumbs in separate shallow bowls. Dredge the hard-boiled egg whites in the flour, then the beaten eggs (allow excess to drip off), then the breadcrumbs, making sure they're coated completely.

Place the Cook & Crisp basket in the pot, press **Air Crisp**, set the temperature to **390°F (199°C)** and allow the Foodi to preheat for **5 minutes**. Set the breaded egg whites in the basket in a single layer and spray with cooking spray. Set the timer to **5 minutes** and press **Start**. Check the egg whites and cook for another **2 to 3 minutes** if needed or until they're browned and the coating is crispy. Lightly spray them with cooking spray a second time if necessary.

Remove them from the basket and place on a serving tray. Pipe the filling into each egg, dividing it evenly.

CRUNCHY AVOCADO WEDGES

SERVES 4

Functions Used
Air Crisp

There are enough Mexican recipes in this book that I thought it needed an easy appetizer that will go well with any one of them. These crispy avocados make an addictive appetizer, but they can also be used to top tacos, a casserole or even as a side to the Chicken Tortilla Soup (page 62).

⅓ cup (42 g) flour

½ tsp coarse salt

2 large eggs, beaten

½ cup (28 g) panko breadcrumbs

2 avocados

In a shallow dish, mix together the flour and salt, then place the beaten eggs into another shallow dish. Do the same with the breadcrumbs. Cut the avocados in half and remove the pits and the skin. Cut each half into 4 wedges. Dredge the avocados in the flour, then in the egg (allowing the excess to drip off), then coat with the breadcrumbs.

Place the Cook & Crisp basket in the pot, press **Air Crisp** and set the temperature to **390°F (199°C)** and allow the Foodi to preheat for **5 minutes**. Place the avocado wedges inside in a single layer, set the timer to **8 minutes** and press **Start**. Cook until they're browned and crispy, turning once halfway through the cooking time.

CAJUN FRIED CHICKEN

SERVES 2 TO 4

Functions Used
Air Crisp

1 cup (125 g) flour

1–2 tbsp (15–30 g) Cajun seasoning

1 tsp coarse salt

1 cup (237 ml) buttermilk

4 bone-in, skin-on chicken thighs (about 1½ lbs [680 g]) (see note)

Cooking spray

Note: The chicken can be soaked in the buttermilk for **1 hour** or up to overnight, if desired. Simply allow the excess to drip off each piece before dipping into the flour mixture.

To me, there's nothing like chicken coated in buttermilk then fried to a golden brown. Although chicken breasts will work here, thighs are more tender and flavorful. I've made these with boneless, skinless thighs as well and they all turn out crispy and delicious!

Mix the flour, Cajun seasoning and salt together in a shallow bowl. Pour the buttermilk into a separate shallow bowl. Dip the chicken thighs into the buttermilk, then the flour mixture, coating each piece thoroughly and shaking off any excess flour.

Place the Cook & Crisp basket in the pot, press **Air Crisp**, set the temperature to **390°F (199°C)** and allow the Foodi to preheat for **5 minutes**. Place the thighs in the basket in a single layer, skin-side up. Spray the tops of the thighs with cooking spray, set the timer to **25 minutes** and press **Start**. Cook until the thighs are cooked through (internal temperature should reach **165°F [74°C]**) and the skin is browned and crispy.

KOREAN CHICKEN WINGS

SERVES 4 TO 6

Functions Used
Air Crisp

If a few of these ingredients are unfamiliar to you, don't let that dissuade you from trying this easy recipe; they're available at most grocery stores and at Asian markets. Gochujang is a paste made from red chiles, and gochugaru is a blend of red pepper flakes. Both add wonderful flavor to Korean food. These wings have won over even my friends and family who swear it's not their favorite cuisine. These are so easy to make and will disappear quickly!

For the Wings
2 lbs (907 g) chicken wings

½ tsp coarse salt

¼ tsp freshly ground black pepper

2 tbsp (30 ml) canola oil (or another oil with a high smoke point)

For the Sauce
3 cloves garlic, minced

2–3 tbsp (50–75 g) gochujang (depending on how spicy you like your chicken wings)

½ tsp gochugaru

2 tbsp (30 ml) soy sauce

1 tsp rice vinegar

2 tbsp (25 g) sugar

2 tbsp (30 ml) water

1 tsp sesame oil

For Toppings
1 tbsp (10 g) sesame seeds

2 green onions, chopped

Season the chicken wings with the salt and pepper. Toss the chicken wings and oil in a large bowl. Place the Cook & Crisp basket in the pot, press **Air Crisp**, set the temperature to **390°F (199°C)** and allow the Foodi to preheat for **5 minutes**. Place the wings inside the basket in a single layer and set the timer to **15 minutes**, then press **Start**.

When the time is up, flip the wings and set the timer for another **10 to 15 minutes** (depending on how crispy you like your wings).

Meanwhile, make the sauce. In a medium saucepan over medium heat, mix together the garlic, gochujang, gochugaru, soy sauce, rice vinegar, sugar, water and sesame oil. Stirring frequently, simmer for **3 to 4 minutes**, until the sugar is dissolved and the sauce is smooth.

Toss the chicken wings with the sauce and place them on a serving platter. Sprinkle with the sesame seeds and green onions.

COCONUT SHRIMP WITH APRICOT DIPPING SAUCE

SERVES 4

Functions Used
Air Crisp

My mom's absolute favorite appetizer is coconut shrimp, so I knew I needed to come up with a recipe that even she would approve of. I've made this recipe for her time and time again—it is a favorite of ours. I was thrilled when I started using my Foodi and realized how quickly I could turn out hot batches of these crispy-yet-tender shrimp!

For the Dipping Sauce
¼ cup (80 g) apricot jam

1 tbsp (16 g) Dijon mustard

1 tsp prepared fresh horseradish

For the Shrimp
3 cups (279 g) unsweetened shredded coconut

½ cup (76 g) cornstarch

1 tsp cayenne pepper

1 tsp coarse salt

4 egg whites, beaten until foamy (beat again as needed)

2 lbs (908 g) medium-sized raw shrimp, peeled with tails on

To make the sauce, heat the apricot jam in the microwave just to soften it (**30 seconds to 1 minute**). In a small bowl, mix the jam, mustard and horseradish. Allow the sauce to sit at room temperature for the flavors to meld while you make the shrimp.

Place the coconut in a blender or food processor. Blend until the coconut is finely chopped (it should still have some texture).

Mix together the cornstarch, cayenne pepper and salt in a shallow dish. Place the beaten egg whites in another dish and the coconut in another. Pat the shrimp dry with paper towels. Dredge the shrimp in the cornstarch mixture, then the egg whites, then the coconut, making sure that the shrimp is generously covered.

Place the Cook & Crisp basket in the pot, press **Air Crisp**, set the temperature to **390°F (199°C)** and allow the Foodi to preheat for **5 minutes**. Place the shrimp in the basket in a single layer (do this in batches if necessary). Set the timer to **3 minutes** and press **Start**.

When the time is up, flip each shrimp and cook for **3 to 4 minutes**, just until the shrimp are cooked through and the coating is crispy. Repeat with the remaining shrimp.

CAJUN PORTOBELLO FRIES WITH LEMON AIOLI

SERVES 4

Functions Used
Air Crisp

Cajun spices and lemon go together like peas and carrots, and these portobello fries are the perfect vessel for that flavor combination. Crispy on the outside, hot and tender on the inside, plus they're a good source of protein!

For the Aioli
⅓ cup (73 g) mayonnaise

1 clove garlic, minced

½ tsp lemon zest

2 tsp (10 ml) fresh lemon juice

Pinch of salt

Two turns of freshly ground black pepper

For the Mushrooms
3 large eggs, beaten

½ cup (62 g) all-purpose flour

1 cup (56 g) panko breadcrumbs

1 tbsp (15 g) Cajun seasoning

Pinch of coarse salt

A few turns of freshly ground black pepper

5 portobello mushroom caps, stems removed and the gills scraped off, then cut into strips (about 6–8 per mushroom, depending on their size)

Cooking spray

To make the aioli, mix together the mayonnaise, garlic, lemon zest, lemon juice, salt and pepper in a small dish. Cover the aioli and set it aside at room temperature while you make the mushrooms.

To make the mushrooms, place the beaten eggs, flour and breadcrumbs in separate shallow dishes. Add the Cajun seasoning, salt and pepper to the flour and mix well. Coat the mushroom slices in the flour mixture, then the egg and lastly the breadcrumbs.

Place the Cook & Crisp basket in the pot, press **Air Crisp** and set the temperature to **390°F (199°C)** and allow the Foodi to preheat for **5 minutes.**

Spray the basket with cooking spray. Place the mushrooms in the basket in a single layer, then spray the tops with cooking spray. Set the timer to **7 minutes** and press **Start**. Cook until they're browned and crispy, turning once halfway through the cooking time. Serve with the aioli for dipping.

CRISPY ROSEMARY POTATO WEDGES

SERVES 2 TO 4

Functions Used
Air Crisp

2 large baking potatoes, unpeeled, cut into 8 wedges each

4 sprigs rosemary, broken or cut into 3–4 pieces each

1 tbsp (15 ml) olive oil

1 tsp coarse sea salt

½ tsp freshly ground black pepper

I'm particular about my roasted potatoes. They need to be soft on the inside and have a good crispy and crunchy outside. The Foodi manages to make them perfectly, and the subtle rosemary flavor paired with the salty fries is perfection! They make a great side dish, appetizer or even a midday snack. They're delicious on their own or dipped into ranch dressing.

Place the potato wedges into a bowl and cover completely with cold water. Let the potatoes sit for at least **30 minutes** and up to **8 hours**. This is an optional step but it helps the potatoes get as crispy as possible.

Drain the potatoes, place them on paper towels and pat them until they're completely dry. Toss the potatoes and rosemary with the oil in a large bowl. Place the Cook & Crisp basket in the pot, press **Air Crisp**, set the temperature to **400°F (204°C)** and allow the Foodi to preheat for **5 minutes**.

Place the potato wedges and rosemary in the basket in a single layer, leaving space around each one if possible, making sure the rosemary is evenly distributed among the potatoes. Sprinkle with the salt and pepper. Set the timer to **10 minutes** and press **Start**.

When the time is up, flip each potato wedge, close the lid and set the timer to **5 minutes**. Remove the potato wedges from the Foodi and serve.

EASY CHICKEN TAQUITOS

SERVES 4 TO 6

Functions Used
Air Crisp

Chipotle chili powder adds a subtle smokiness to these easy taquitos that makes them extra flavorful! Feel free to use all chili powder if that's what you have on hand—they'll still be delicious. Pepper Jack cheese also makes a great alternative if you want to spice these up!

½ tsp garlic powder

1½ tsp (4 g) chili powder

½ tsp chipotle chili powder

1 tsp ground cumin

½ tsp coarse salt

¼ tsp freshly ground black pepper

2½ cups (350 g) cooked, shredded chicken

1½ cups (181 g) shredded Mexican-blend cheese

12 (6-inch [15-cm]) corn tortillas

Cooking spray

In a medium-sized mixing bowl, mix together the garlic powder, chili powder, chipotle chili powder, cumin, salt and pepper. Add the chicken and use your hands to gently mix the chicken in the seasoning until it's fully and evenly coated. Mix in the cheese.

Place the tortillas between damp paper towels and microwave for **1 minute**, just to soften.

Divide the chicken mixture evenly among the tortillas and roll up each tightly. Place the Cook & Crisp basket in the pot, press **Air Crisp**, set the temperature to **390°F (199°C)** and allow the Foodi to preheat for **5 minutes**.

Place half the taquitos seam-side down in the basket in a single layer (do this in batches if necessary). Spray the taquitos with cooking spray. Set the timer to **7 minutes** and press **Start**. When the time is up, flip each taquito and cook for **5 minutes**, or until they're lightly browned and crispy. Repeat with the rest of the taquitos.

SAUSAGE & PEPPER CALZONES

SERVES 4

Functions Used
Sear/Saute, Air Crisp

1 lb (454 g) ground Italian sausage

½ cup (75 g) red bell peppers, chopped

1 lb (454 g) uncooked prepared pizza dough

¼ cup (62 g) pizza sauce, plus more for serving

1 cup (121 g) shredded mozzarella cheese

1 cup (246 g) ricotta cheese

1 egg, beaten

Cooking spray

We make calzones so often that my kids are now in charge of putting these together. I'll often pick up different toppings and let everyone load their own, but this version is everyone's favorite. The Foodi gives these calzones a perfectly browned, crispy crust and a hot, gooey center. Why pay for takeout when you can have hot, cheesy calzones in even less time?

Press **Sear/Saute** and set the heat to **Medium**. Allow the Foodi to preheat for **5 minutes**. Place the sausage in the pot and cook until almost no pink remains, about **5 minutes**. Add the bell peppers and cook until starting to soften, about **3 minutes**. Remove the sausage mixture from the pot with a slotted spoon and clean out the pot (use caution, as the pot may still be hot).

Divide the pizza dough equally into 4 pieces, then roll each piece into a circle, about ¼ inch (6 mm) thick. Spread 1 tablespoon (15 g) pizza sauce onto each dough circle, then top each with ¼ cup (30 g) mozzarella and ¼ cup (61 g) ricotta. Top with the sausage mixture, dividing it evenly. Fold the dough over and pinch to seal the edges, then lightly brush each calzone with the egg.

Place the Cook & Crisp basket into the pot, press **Air Crisp**, set the temperature to **390°F (199°C)** and allow the Foodi to preheat for **5 minutes**.

Set 2 calzones in the basket and spray them with cooking spray. Set the timer to **8 minutes** and press **Start**. Flip the calzones after **4 minutes** and spray them again with cooking spray. When the time is up, remove the calzones and repeat the process with the remaining 2 calzones. Serve with the extra pizza sauce on the side.

MOM'S ITALIAN MEATBALLS

SERVES 4

Functions Used
Air Crisp

You guessed it—this is my mom's recipe that she's used since before I was born. She likes to use all beef, and it might not be traditional, but it's definitely delicious. We usually eat these as-is with a side of marinara for dipping. She'll sometimes freeze them to use later for spaghetti night. Cooking these in the Foodi means less time and no flipping each meatball!

2 lbs (907 g) 90% lean ground beef (or a combination of beef, pork and/or veal)

2 cloves garlic, minced

2 large eggs

2 cups (118 g) crumbled day-old white bread

1 cup (237 ml) milk, room temperature, plus more if needed

1 cup (100 g) grated Parmesan cheese

2 tbsp (5 g) chopped parsley, plus more for garnish

1 tsp coarse salt

¼ tsp freshly ground black pepper

Cooking spray

In a large bowl, mix together the ground beef, garlic and eggs. Soak the bread in the milk for at least **5 minutes**, then mix it with the ground beef mixture. Add the Parmesan, chopped parsley, salt and pepper; mix it until it's just combined. Once it's all mixed together, add a small amount of milk (1 to 2 tablespoons [15 to 30 ml] at a time) if the mixture is too dry. Divide the mixture into 1-inch (2.5-cm) portions, rolling each with your hands into a round meatball shape, about 32 meatballs total.

Place the Cook & Crisp basket in the pot, press **Air Crisp**, set the temperature to **390°F (199°C)** and allow the Foodi to preheat for **5 minutes**. Spray the basket with cooking spray. Place the meatballs inside the basket in a single layer and spray the tops with cooking spray. You'll need to cook the meatballs in batches. Set the timer to **10 minutes** and press **Start**. When the time is up, check that the meatballs are cooked through; cook another couple of minutes if necessary. Repeat with the remaining meatballs until they are all cooked. Garnish with extra parsley if you'd like.

BUFFALO CHICKEN EMPANADAS

SERVES 4

Functions Used
Air Crisp

These are far from traditional empanadas, but the flavor is so good that I know you won't mind! I keep prepared empanada dough discs stocked in the freezer to pull out on busy nights. The filling keeps for a few days in the fridge, so sometimes I make only the filling so we can cook just a few empanadas at a time for whoever's hungry. The Foodi creates a crispy brown crust and a hot, creamy filling!

1½ cups (210 g) cooked, shredded chicken

¼ cup (61 g) buffalo sauce (such as Frank's Red Hot), plus more for serving

¼ cup (60 g) cream cheese, softened

2 tbsp (17 g) crumbled blue cheese (optional)

1 refrigerated pie crust (or empanada dough discs, "discos," usually in the frozen section)

Cooking spray

Mix together the chicken, buffalo sauce, cream cheese and blue cheese (if using) in a medium-sized mixing bowl. Cut out 8 circles from the refrigerated pie crust, or as many circles as you can with a cookie or biscuit cutter (cooking time will be the same). Divide the filling evenly among the circles, spreading the filling on one side. Make sure to avoid overfilling, and leave a border around the filling. Fold the dough over and crimp the edges with a fork.

Place the Cook & Crisp basket in the pot, press **Air Crisp**, set the temperature to **350°F (177°C)** and allow the Foodi to preheat for **5 minutes**. Spray the basket with the cooking spray. Place the empanadas inside in a single layer (do this in batches if necessary) and spray the tops with cooking spray. Set the timer to **8 minutes**, then press **Start**. Halfway through cooking time, flip the empanadas, spray the other side with cooking spray and complete the cooking process until they're golden brown. Serve with extra buffalo sauce for dipping.

Note: You can fill these empanadas with just about anything! Use barbecue sauce in place of the buffalo sauce, use cooked beef taco meat and shredded cheese, or even ham with Swiss cheese.

EASY SPANAKOPITA

SERVES 4 TO 6

Functions Used
Sear/Saute, Air Crisp

2 tsp (10 ml) extra-virgin olive oil

1 small onion, diced

1 clove garlic, minced

1 (10-oz [282-g]) package frozen spinach, thawed (squeeze out as much water as possible with a dry kitchen towel)

1 cup (121 g) crumbled feta cheese

1 large egg, beaten

½ tsp coarse salt

¼ tsp freshly ground black pepper

16 sheets frozen phyllo dough

¼ cup (60 g) butter, melted

Cooking spray

Greek food is one of my favorites, and spanakopita is at the top of my list. The tender filling and crunchy bite from the phyllo is irresistible to me. Make these for dinner, an appetizer or for a party. The Foodi turns the phyllo dough into a perfectly browned and crunchy top!

Press **Sear/Saute** and set the heat to **Medium**. Allow the Foodi to preheat for **5 minutes**.

Add the oil to the pot and when it's shimmering, add the onion. Cook until the onion is soft, **4 to 5 minutes**. Add the garlic and cook for **1 minute**, stirring frequently. Add the spinach and cook, stirring occasionally, until most of the water has evaporated from the spinach, about **2 minutes**. Stir in the feta cheese, egg, salt and pepper, then set the filling aside and wipe out the pot.

Remove the phyllo sheets from the package and place them on a damp towel. Take out 2 sheets then immediately place another damp towel on top of the remaining sheets to keep them from drying out (they dry out very fast otherwise).

Keeping the 2 sheets together, brush the sheets with the melted butter; brush just the top one and it will coat both. Cut into 4 pieces, then place 1 tablespoon (15 g) of the filling in one corner and fold it diagonally. Keep folding until you reach the end of the strip, then tuck in the end. Continue this process with the remaining filling and phyllo sheets, then brush the tops of the triangles with any remaining butter.

Place the Cook & Crisp basket in the pot, press **Air Crisp**, set the temperature to **375°F (191°C)** and allow the Foodi to preheat for **5 minutes**. Spray the basket with cooking spray. Working in batches, place the spanakopita inside in a single layer, then spray the tops of the spanakopita with cooking spray. Set the timer to **12 minutes**, then press **Start**. Cook until they're lightly browned and crispy. Repeat with the remaining spanakopita.

RIB-EYES WITH COMPOUND BUTTER

SERVES 2

Functions Used
Air Crisp

Making steaks in your Foodi couldn't be easier or faster! Choose your favorite compound butter flavor and keep it on hand for a quick but delicious weeknight entrée. My personal favorites are the Blue Cheese Butter or the Truffle Butter, but all are delicious! You'll have leftover compound butter, so either save it to make more steaks, or try spreading it on warm bread or tossing it with roasted vegetables. You can cut the compound butter recipes in half if you prefer not to have any extra.

2 bone-in rib-eye steaks, about 2 lbs (907 g), room temperature

1 tsp coarse salt

½ tsp freshly ground black pepper

Cooking spray

Compound butter, for serving (see following recipes)

Garlic Herb Butter
½ cup (120 g) high-quality unsalted butter, softened

2 cloves garlic, minced

1 tbsp (3 g) chopped fresh oregano

1 tbsp (3 g) chopped fresh rosemary

1 tbsp (3 g) chopped fresh chives

¼ tsp coarse salt

¼ tsp freshly ground black pepper

Chipotle Butter
½ cup (120 g) high-quality unsalted butter, softened

1½ tbsp (10 g) seeded and minced chipotle pepper

2 tsp (10 ml) fresh lime juice

¼ tsp coarse salt

Tarragon Butter
½ cup (120 g) high-quality unsalted butter, softened

2–3 tbsp (6–9 g) finely chopped fresh tarragon

2 tbsp (25 g) finely minced onion

1 clove garlic, finely minced

½ tsp lemon zest

¼ tsp coarse salt

½ tsp freshly ground black pepper

Blue Cheese Butter
½ cup (120 g) high-quality unsalted butter, softened

½ cup (60 g) blue cheese or gorgonzola (or to taste)

¼ tsp coarse salt

⅛ tsp freshly ground black pepper

Truffle Butter
½ cup (120 g) high-quality unsalted butter, softened

1 tbsp (8 g) grated truffles (or to taste)

½ tsp coarse salt

Make the compound butter first so it can chill. The method for each flavor is the same. Place the softened butter into a mixing bowl then add the other ingredients. Stir well to make sure the ingredients are evenly incorporated. Place a sheet of parchment or waxed paper on a flat surface. Dollop the butter in the center of the paper as close to a log shape as you can. Fold up the sides of the paper and use your hands to press the butter into a log. Twist the ends of the paper. Refrigerate the butter for **30 minutes**, then re-form into a log if necessary. Place the butter in the freezer for **1 hour**.

Place the Cook & Crisp basket in the pot, press **Air Crisp**, set the temperature to **390°F (199°C)** and allow the Foodi to preheat for **5 minutes**. Rub the steaks with the salt and pepper. Spray the basket with cooking spray, then place the steaks inside. Set the timer to **10 minutes**, then press **Start**.

After **5 minutes**, flip the steaks and continue cooking for **5 minutes**. This will yield a medium-rare steak, but it's best to check it with a meat thermometer since the thickness varies. Remove the steaks from the Foodi when they reach **130°F (54°C)**, then tent them with aluminum foil and let them rest for **5 minutes**. The internal temperature will rise another 5 degrees while resting. Place a slice of the compound butter on top of each steak before serving.

*See photo on page 70.

Note: These steaks are delicious paired with Crispy Rosemary Potato Wedges (page 89).

CRUNCHY BUFFALO CHICKPEAS

SERVES 4

Functions Used
Air Crisp

2 (15-oz [425-g]) cans chickpeas (garbanzo beans)

2 tbsp (30 g) butter, melted

⅓ cup (82 g) buffalo sauce (such as Frank's Red Hot)

1 tsp garlic powder

½ tsp coarse salt

Cooking spray

I can usually take chickpeas or leave 'em, but when they're crunchy with so much flavor, I'll always take 'em! These are so easy to make, are a fairly healthy snack and everyone loves them. They're great on their own as a snack but are equally delicious added to a salad. I've even used them to top stuffed avocados!

Drain the chickpeas and pat them dry thoroughly with paper towels. Mix together the butter, buffalo sauce, garlic powder and salt in a medium-sized mixing bowl. Add the chickpeas and mix well, making sure all the chickpeas are coated.

Place the Cook & Crisp basket in the pot, press **Air Crisp**, set the temperature to **390°F (199°C)** and allow the Foodi to preheat for **5 minutes**. Spray the basket with cooking spray, then place the chickpeas inside. Set the timer to **20 minutes** and press **Start**. Every **5 minutes**, open the lid and shake or stir the chickpeas. Continue cooking until the sauce is baked on and they're crispy.

FAST & HEALTHY

Our culture today is filled with fast everything—we want it now and just how we want it. But getting a healthy meal on the table fast isn't always easy or possible. The Foodi is a huge timesaver that makes healthy meals so much simpler and quicker! My go-to is fish with asparagus since it cooks quickly and all at the same time. But as someone who doesn't care to eat the same meal over and over, I came up with some delicious yet quick and healthy options, all made even easier with the Foodi.

My Three Favorites

GARLIC ITALIAN CHICKEN BREASTS WITH BELL PEPPERS & BROCCOLI

SERVES 4

Functions Used
Air Crisp

2 tsp (2 g) Italian seasoning

½ tsp garlic powder

¼ tsp onion powder

½ tsp coarse salt

¼ tsp freshly ground black pepper

3 tbsp (45 ml) extra-virgin olive oil

4 boneless, skinless chicken breasts, cut into bite-sized pieces

1 cup (100 g) chopped broccoli (small, bite-sized pieces)

1 red bell pepper, chopped

A healthy meal doesn't get much simpler than this, and it all comes together in just 10 minutes' cooking time! Serve this flavorful meal over rice or a salad.

Mix together the Italian seasoning, garlic powder, onion powder, salt and pepper in a small dish. Stir in the oil. Place the chicken, broccoli and bell pepper in a large resealable plastic bag. Pour the oil mixture into the bag, seal it and gently shake the bag to ensure everything is coated with the spices.

Place the Cook & Crisp basket in the pot, press **Air Crisp**, set the temperature to **400°F (204°C)** and allow the Foodi to preheat for **5 minutes**. Pour the chicken and vegetable mixture inside the pot. Set the timer to **10 minutes** and press **Start**. Cook until the chicken is cooked through (internal temperature should reach **165°F [74°C]**) and the vegetables are tender.

STUFFED RED BELL PEPPERS

SERVES 4

Functions Used
Sear/Saute, Pressure Cook

1 lb (454 g) lean ground beef or turkey

½ medium onion, chopped

2 cloves garlic, minced

1 tbsp (3 g) Italian seasoning

1 cup (245 g) tomato sauce

1 tsp Worcestershire sauce

1 (14.5-oz [411-g]) can fire-roasted diced tomatoes, drained

3 ears fresh corn, kernels removed and cobs discarded

1 cup (197 g) cooked white or brown rice

1 tsp coarse salt

¼ tsp freshly ground black pepper

4 large red bell peppers, tops cut off, seeds and membrane removed

Whenever I have leftover rice, this is the recipe I turn to. It's healthy, super tasty and a great way to get more veggies into my family's diet. On the rare occasion we have a leftover stuffed pepper, I like to chop it up and serve it as a salad over spinach; it's amazing!

Press **Sear/Saute** and set the heat to **Medium**. Allow the Foodi to preheat for **5 minutes**.

Add the beef or turkey to the pot and cook for about **5 minutes**, stirring occasionally until no pink remains. Add the onion and cook for a few minutes, just until it's softened. Add the garlic and Italian seasoning and cook **1 minute**, stirring frequently. Add the tomato sauce, Worcestershire, diced tomatoes, corn kernels and rice to the pot and stir to combine. Season with the salt and pepper.

Place the beef mixture in a large bowl, clean out the pot, then return the pot to the base. Fill each bell pepper with the beef mixture, then set each filled bell pepper inside the pot. Spoon any additional filling onto the tops of the bell peppers. Place the pressure lid onto the pot and make sure the valve is set to **Seal**. Press **Pressure** and set to **HI**. Set the timer to **10 minutes**, then press **Start**.

When the time is up, carefully release the pressure by turning the valve to **Vent**. When all of the pressure is released, open the lid and place each bell pepper on a serving plate.

CAULIFLOWER STEAKS WITH CHIMICHURRI

SERVES 2 TO 4

Functions Used
Air Crisp

My partner, Rob, has eaten exclusively Keto for the last two years, so I try to come up with as many low-carb recipes as possible. I make cauliflower steaks often, and the pairing with tangy chimichurri makes these a real treat! This will serve two people as a main dish or four as a side dish. If you can only find a medium- or large-sized cauliflower, simply cut it to size and reserve any extra for another meal.

For the Chimichurri Sauce
½ cup (118 ml) extra-virgin olive oil

1 cup (40 g) fresh Italian parsley leaves

1 large clove garlic

2 tbsp (5 g) fresh oregano leaves

1 large pinch red pepper flakes

2 tbsp (30 ml) red wine vinegar

½ tsp coarse salt

¼ tsp freshly ground black pepper

For the Cauliflower Steaks
1 small head cauliflower, about 1 lb (454 g)

1 tbsp (15 ml) extra-virgin olive oil

1 tsp coarse salt

To make the chimichurri sauce, place the oil, parsley, garlic, oregano, red pepper flakes, vinegar, salt and pepper in a high-powered blender. Blend until very smooth. Allow the sauce to sit at room temperature while you make the steaks to allow the flavors to meld.

Trim the cauliflower stem and remove the leaves, leaving the core intact. Turn the cauliflower upright and slice it into four 1-inch (2.5-cm)-thick "steaks." Brush the cauliflower steaks with the oil and season them with the salt.

Place the Cook & Crisp basket in the pot, press **Air Crisp**, set the temperature to **375°F (191°C)** and allow the Foodi to preheat for **5 minutes**. Place the cauliflower steaks in the basket in a single layer, leaning them against the side if necessary. Set the timer to **15 minutes**. Flip the steaks halfway through cooking time. Place the steaks on a serving platter and top with the chimichurri.

GARLIC PORK LOIN WITH BLUE CHEESE MASHED POTATOES

SERVES 4 TO 6

Functions Used
Pressure Cook

You'll love the ease of this complete meal in your Foodi! If you don't care for the flavor of blue cheese, feel free to omit it entirely or substitute it with Parmesan, Cheddar or even pepper Jack. The chicken stock in this recipe replaces heavy cream and butter, making this dish flavorful but with less fat and calories.

1 tbsp (15 ml) extra-virgin olive oil

2 tbsp (19 g) minced garlic

1 tbsp (3 g) Italian seasoning

2 lbs (907 g) pork loin

1 cup (237 ml) chicken stock or broth

3 lbs (1.4 kg) red potatoes, cut in half if very large

½ cup (60 g) crumbled blue cheese

¾ tsp coarse salt

¼ tsp freshly ground black pepper

Mix together the oil, garlic and Italian seasoning in a small dish. Rub the mixture all over the pork loin and set aside.

Pour the chicken stock into the pot, then place the potatoes directly into the broth. Place the pork loin on top of the potatoes. Place the pressure lid onto the pot and make sure the valve is set to **Seal**. Press **Pressure** and set to **HI**. Set the timer to **30 minutes**, then press **Start**.

When the time is up, release the pressure by carefully moving the valve to **Vent**. When all the pressure is released, remove the roast from the pot, leaving behind the potatoes and stock. Set the roast on a cutting or carving board to rest.

Using a potato masher, mash the potatoes until they reach your desired consistency. Add the blue cheese and stir to combine. Season the potatoes with the salt and pepper, then slice the roast.

BROWN SUGAR & MUSTARD SALMON

SERVES 4

Functions Used
Air Crisp

4 salmon filets (about 1½ lbs [675 g])

2 tsp (10 g) coarse salt, divided

½ cup (125 g) Dijon mustard

¼ cup (45 g) brown sugar

½ lb (227 g) asparagus, cut into 1-inch (2.5-cm) pieces

1 tsp extra-virgin olive oil

Cooking spray

2 tbsp (5 g) chopped parsley (optional)

My daughter Kylie is obsessed with salmon, and since it's a healthy dinner choice, I try to come up with new ways to serve it. This easy glaze is a family favorite; it's slightly sweet with a little bite from the mustard. The fact that the asparagus is done at the same time is just a bonus!

Season the salmon with ½ teaspoon of salt. Mix together the mustard and brown sugar and brush it onto the salmon. Toss the asparagus with the oil and the remaining salt. Place the Cook & Crisp basket in the pot, press **Air Crisp**, set the temperature to **390°F (199°C)** and allow the Foodi to preheat for **5 minutes**.

Spray the basket with cooking spray. Place the salmon inside in a single layer, then place the asparagus around and between the salmon. Set the timer to **5 minutes** and press **Start**. When the time is up, check the salmon and asparagus to make sure the salmon is cooked through and the asparagus is tender, adding another minute of cooking time if necessary. Sprinkle with chopped parsley before serving if you'd like.

SALMON CAKES WITH SRIRACHA AIOLI

SERVES 2 TO 3

Functions Used
Air Crisp

Canned salmon is one of my pantry staples since it can quickly become a tasty meal with little effort. Prior to owning a Ninja Foodi, I'd have to heat the oven if I didn't want the extra calories from frying. But now I have the best of both worlds—no heating my oven, the salmon cakes are still fried and I get dinner on the table faster than ever!

1 (14.75-oz [418-g]) can salmon, drained

1 large egg

⅓ cup (40 g) breadcrumbs

¼ tsp garlic powder

¼ tsp coarse salt

¼ tsp freshly ground pepper

½ cup (110 g) mayonnaise

1–2 tsp (5–10 g) sriracha (to taste)

1 tbsp (15 ml) extra-virgin olive oil

½ lemon, sliced into wedges (for garnish and squeezing over salmon patties)

Mix together the salmon, egg, breadcrumbs, garlic powder, salt and pepper in a medium bowl. Place in the refrigerator for **15 minutes**.

Meanwhile, mix the mayonnaise and sriracha together in a small dish. Allow it to sit at room temperature until the patties are ready.

Form the salmon mixture into 4 to 6 patties, depending on how big you want them (cooking time will be the same). Gently brush both sides of the patties with the oil or spray them with cooking spray. Place the Cook & Crisp basket in the pot, press **Air Crisp**, set the temperature to **390°F (199°C)** and allow the Foodi to preheat for **5 minutes**.

Place the patties inside the basket in a single layer (they should all fit at once). Set the timer to **8 minutes** and press **Start**. When the time is up, serve the salmon patties with a dollop of sriracha aioli and a lemon wedge.

BAKED TILAPIA WITH ASPARAGUS

SERVES 4

Functions Used
Bake/Roast

4 tilapia filets, about 1½ lbs (675 g) total

½ tsp coarse salt

¼ tsp freshly ground black pepper

8 cloves garlic, minced

½ cup (120 g) butter, sliced into 12 squares

8 lemon slices

1 lb (454 g) thin asparagus stalks, trimmed and cut into thirds

This is a recipe I make all the time when we're camping or if the weather is too hot to turn on the oven. It's so nice not to have much clean-up! Try adding halved cherry tomatoes to the packets for another flavor twist.

Place each tilapia filet on a piece of aluminum foil or parchment paper large enough to fold and enclose tightly. Season each filet with the salt and pepper. Divide the remaining ingredients by four. Top the tilapia filets with the garlic, then the butter and lemon slices. Add the asparagus to the packets, then fold and seal the packets and place them inside the pot.

Close the crisping lid. Press **Bake/Roast** and set the temperature to **400°F (204°C)** and the timer to **10 minutes**. Press **Start**. Bake for **10 minutes**, or until the tilapia is cooked through and flakes easily with a fork. Serve in the foil packets or remove and place on serving plates.

BLACKENED SALMON WITH ROASTED TOMATOES & GREEN BEANS

SERVES 4

Functions Used
Air Crisp

2 tbsp (30 g) butter, melted

2 tbsp (30 g) blackening or Cajun seasoning

4 salmon filets

1 cup (150 g) cherry tomatoes

½ lb (227 g) green beans

2 tsp (10 ml) extra-virgin olive oil, plus a little extra for tomatoes

¼ tsp coarse salt

The spicy seasoning on this salmon is the perfect balance to the sweet tomatoes and earthy green beans. It's an easy and healthy weeknight meal, plus you can use a non-spicy seasoning blend for anyone who doesn't care for spiciness.

Line the fryer basket with aluminum foil (optional but makes for easier cleanup). Mix together the butter and blackening seasoning. Coat the salmon on all sides with the butter mixture.

Place the Cook & Crisp basket into the pot, press **Air Crisp**, set the temperature to **390°F (199°C)** and allow the Foodi to preheat for **5 minutes**. Place the salmon in the pot, then place the cherry tomatoes and green beans around the salmon. Drizzle lightly with the oil and sprinkle the tomatoes and green beans with the salt. Set the timer to **7 minutes** and press **Start**. Cook for 7 minutes, or until the salmon is cooked through and the green beans are crisp-tender.

CHICKEN & CORN CASSEROLE

SERVES 4

Functions Used
Sear/Saute, Bake/Roast

I can't stress enough how amazing fresh corn is in this flavorful casserole, but if none is available, it's still delicious with frozen. I try to make dishes that make great leftovers, and this one definitely fits that bill. Although we usually don't have any left—it's that good!

1 tbsp (15 ml) extra-virgin olive oil

½ medium sweet onion, chopped

3 cloves garlic, minced

2 tsp (10 g) chili powder

1 tsp ancho chili powder

2 cups (300 g) fresh or frozen corn

2 cups (251 g) cooked, chopped chicken

1 cup (121 g) shredded low-fat Mexican-style cheese, divided

1 (14.5-oz [411-g]) can fire-roasted diced tomatoes, with liquid

1 (8-oz [227-g]) can tomato sauce

3 cups (591 g) cooked rice

½ tsp salt

¼ tsp freshly ground black pepper

½ cup (10 g) chopped cilantro, for serving

2 green onions, chopped, for serving

½ cup (110 g) low-fat sour cream, for serving

Press **Sear/Saute** and set the heat to **Medium**. Allow the Foodi to preheat for **5 minutes**. Add the oil and when it's shimmering, add the onion and cook, stirring occasionally, until it starts to soften, about **5 minutes**. Add the garlic, chili powder and ancho chili powder; cook about **1 minute**.

Add the corn, chicken, ½ cup (60 g) of the cheese, diced tomatoes, tomato sauce, rice, salt and pepper; mix well. Sprinkle with the remaining cheese. Press **Bake/Roast**, then set the temperature to **350°F (177°C)** and the timer to **15 minutes**. Press **Start**. Bake until it's bubbling and the cheese is melted. Sprinkle with the chopped cilantro and green onions, and serve with the sour cream.

CHICKEN SAUSAGE & VEGGIES

SERVES 4

Functions Used
Air Crisp

1 (12-oz [340-g]) package chicken sausage, sliced crosswise into bite-sized pieces (any flavor)

2 tbsp (30 ml) extra-virgin olive oil

¼ medium sweet onion, chopped

1 red bell pepper, chopped

1 poblano pepper, chopped

2 ears fresh corn, kernels removed and cobs discarded

1 cup (150 g) cherry tomatoes, halved

½ tsp coarse salt

¼ tsp freshly ground black pepper

There's a small amount of chopping for this recipe, but since you can skip sauteing and instead just toss it all together then let your Foodi do the work, it's still one that's quick, flavorful and healthy. Any sausage will work, but I've found that chicken sausage lends so much flavor that we like to skip the added fat and calories of pork sausage.

Toss all of the ingredients together in a large mixing bowl.

Place the Cook & Crisp basket in the pot, press **Air Crisp**, set the temperature to **390°F (199°C)** and allow the Foodi to preheat for **5 minutes**. Place the sausage mixture inside. Set the timer to **10 minutes** and press **Start**. Cook until the sausage and vegetables are cooked through, stirring halfway through the cooking time.

BALSAMIC & MUSTARD-GLAZED CHICKEN THIGHS

SERVES 4

Functions Used
Air Crisp

This sticky glaze is sweet and flavorful, plus it takes just a minute to throw together. We'll enjoy these chicken thighs with rice and a vegetable, or I'll cut them up and use them in salads. Using skinless thighs means less fat and calories but they're just as flavorful with the sweet sauce!

2 tbsp (30 ml) balsamic vinegar

2 tbsp (30 ml) honey

1 clove garlic, minced

1 tbsp (15 ml) Dijon mustard

4 boneless, skinless chicken thighs, about 1½ lbs (675 g) total

½ tsp coarse salt

¼ tsp freshly ground black pepper

Cooking spray

Mix the vinegar, honey, garlic and mustard together in a small dish. Season the chicken thighs with salt and pepper. Brush the thighs with half of the vinegar mixture. Place the Cook & Crisp basket in the pot, press **Air Crisp**, set the temperature to **390°F (199°C)** and allow the Foodi to preheat for **5 minutes**.

Spray the basket with cooking spray, then place the chicken thighs inside. Set the timer to **14 minutes**. Press **Start**. Halfway through the cooking time, flip the thighs and brush them with the remaining vinegar mixture. When the cooking time is up, check to ensure the thighs are completely cooked (internal temperature should reach **165°F [74°C]**), adding another minute if necessary. Remove the thighs and serve immediately.

TURKEY & CABBAGE SOUP

SERVES 4 TO 6

Functions Used
Sear/Saute, Pressure Cook

2 tsp (10 ml) extra-virgin olive oil

½ medium onion, chopped

2 medium carrots, peeled and chopped

2 cloves garlic, minced

2 tsp (2 g) Italian seasoning

1 lb (454 g) ground turkey

1 lb (454 g) green cabbage, coarsely chopped

1 cup (211 g) long-grain white rice

4 cups (946 ml) chicken broth

2 (14.5-oz [411-g]) cans fire-roasted diced tomatoes

¼ tsp crushed red pepper flakes (optional)

1 tsp coarse salt

¼ tsp freshly ground black pepper

This healthy yet hearty soup is perfect for the cold-weather months. It's a complete meal with lean meat, vegetables and rice, all in one pot! Fresh or frozen cauliflower rice can be used in place of the white rice for an even healthier, low-carb meal.

Press **Sear/Saute** and set the heat to **Medium**. Allow the Foodi to preheat for **5 minutes**.

Add the oil and when it's shimmering, add the onion and carrots. Cook for about **5 minutes**, stirring frequently. Stir in the garlic and Italian seasoning and cook for **1 minute**.

Add the ground turkey, stirring to break it up. Cook for about **5 minutes** or until almost no pink remains. Add the cabbage, rice, chicken broth and tomatoes to the pot. Place the pressure lid onto the pot and make sure the valve is set to **Seal**. Press **Pressure** and set to **HI**. Set the timer to **15 minutes**, then press **Start**.

When the time is up, carefully release the pressure by turning the pressure valve to **Vent**. When all the pressure is released, remove the pressure lid and stir the soup. Stir in the red pepper flakes (if using), salt and pepper.

GOAT CHEESE, SPINACH & SUN-DRIED TOMATO HASSELBACK CHICKEN

SERVES 4

Functions Used
Bake/Roast

4 medium-sized chicken breasts, about 1½ lbs (675 g)

½ tsp coarse salt

¼ tsp freshly ground black pepper

2–4 oz (56–113 g) goat cheese

1–2 cups (30–60 g) loosely packed fresh spinach

¼–½ cup (37–75 g) julienned oil-packed sun-dried tomatoes

I used to avoid stuffing chicken breasts because the filling always oozed out and it was more hassle than I wanted on a busy night. This method is so simple, however, that now I stuff chicken all the time. The filling stays much better when you cut slits through the chicken vs. a pocket, and the combination of goat cheese, spinach and sun-dried tomatoes adds so much flavor too!

Cut 5 to 6 slits crosswise in each chicken breast, taking care not to cut all the way through. Season the chicken with the salt and pepper. Place an ounce (28 g) of the goat cheese into the slits of each chicken breast, dividing it evenly. Do the same with the spinach and sun-dried tomatoes.

Place the chicken breasts in the pot, then press **Bake/Roast** and set the temperature to **400°F (204°C)** and the timer to **20 minutes**. Press **Start**. When the time is up, check to ensure the chicken is cooked through (internal temperature should reach **165°F [74°C]**).

BASIL PESTO CHICKEN BITES

SERVES 4

Functions Used
Air Crisp

If you're looking for the perfect party appetizer, you've found it. Pop toothpicks into the chicken bites and watch these disappear before anything else! The fresh pesto combined with the tender, air-fried chicken bites is irresistible! These delicious bites will also make a delightful main dish when paired with a simple salad.

For the Basil Pesto
1 cup (40 g) basil (lightly packed)

2 tbsp (16 g) pine nuts

1 clove garlic

⅓ cup (79 ml) high-quality extra-virgin olive oil

½ tsp coarse salt

¼ tsp freshly ground black pepper

⅔ cup (66 g) shredded Parmesan cheese

For the Chicken Bites
2 lbs (907 g) ground chicken (or turkey)

2 large eggs

3 cloves garlic, minced

½ cup (60 g) breadcrumbs

1 tsp salt

½ tsp freshly ground black pepper

Cooking spray

To make the pesto, place all the pesto ingredients except the Parmesan in a food processor or high-powered blender. Blend on high until it's very smooth. Add the Parmesan and blend it again until it's smooth.

To make the chicken, using your hands, mix together the ground chicken, eggs, garlic, breadcrumbs, salt and black pepper. Form the mixture into small, bite-sized rounds, about 1 inch (2.5 cm) thick. Place the Cook & Crisp basket in the pot, press **Air Crisp**, set the temperature to **375°F (191°C)** and allow the Foodi to preheat for **5 minutes**.

Spray the basket with cooking spray, then place the chicken bites inside in a single layer (do this in two batches), then spray the bites with more cooking spray. Set the timer to **14 minutes** and press **Start**. Cook the chicken bites until they're cooked through, flipping once halfway through the cooking time.

Serve the chicken bites on a platter with a small bowl of the pesto for dipping. Alternatively, you can pour some pesto into a shallow dish, set the chicken bites on top and serve the remaining pesto on the side.

QUICK & DELICIOUS SIDE DISHES

The side dish is often an afterthought, but it doesn't have to be. Even simple side dishes can be flavorful and beloved. The Foodi is spectacular for turning simple broccoli into a charred delight, and fresh sweet corn can be made into an amazing dish with a few simple toppings! A few of these recipes could double as an appetizer or even a main dish, so try them all and pick your personal favorites.

My Three Favorites

Green Bean & Blue Cheese Casserole (page 142)

Mexican Street Corn (Elote) (page 145)

Charred Broccoli with Garlic & Parmesan (page 150)

TWICE BAKED POTATOES

SERVES 4

Functions Used
Air Crisp

2 large russet potatoes

1 tbsp (15 ml) canola oil

2 oz (57 g) cream cheese, softened

2 tbsp (30 g) butter, softened

½ cup (110 g) sour cream

¼ cup (59 ml) milk

½ tsp coarse salt

¼ tsp freshly ground black pepper

½ cup (60 g) shredded Cheddar cheese, divided

4 oz (113 g) bacon, cooked until crisp then crumbled

2 tbsp (6 g) chopped green onions or chives

"Baking" potatoes in the air fryer is the only way I'll prepare them after using my Foodi. Sometimes I don't bother with baking them twice, but when I want to make a dish my family will really rave over, I take the few extra steps to turn them into creamy, cheesy potato perfection.

Prick each potato a few times each with a fork. Rub the outside of each potato with a small amount of oil. Place the trivet in the pot and place the potatoes directly on the trivet. Press **Air Crisp**, set the temperature to **375°F (191°C)** and the timer to **40 minutes**.

When the potatoes are done, slice each potato in half lengthwise, then gently scoop out the potato into a medium-sized mixing bowl, leaving a thin potato shell. Add the cream cheese, butter, sour cream, milk, salt and pepper, mixing it until it's smooth and creamy.

Scoop the mixture back into the potato shells. Top with the cheese and bacon crumbles, then place the potatoes back in the basket. Press **Air Crisp**, set the temperature to **375°F (191°C)** and the timer to **8 minutes**. Cook the potatoes for **8 minutes**, or until the filling is heated through and the cheese is melted. Top with the chopped green onions and serve.

PARMESAN ROASTED CAULIFLOWER WITH MARINARA

SERVES 4

Functions Used
Air Crisp

1 medium head cauliflower, broken or cut into small florets

2 tbsp (30 ml) extra-virgin olive oil

½ tsp coarse salt

¼ tsp freshly ground black pepper

¼ cup (25 g) grated Parmesan cheese

½ cup (123 g) marinara sauce, for dipping

The beauty of this recipe is that you can make it just how you like it. Plus, it's low-carb, and even non-cauliflower lovers have been won over by this dish! The smaller the florets, the crispier pieces you'll get, so take the time to cut down your bigger florets.

Toss the cauliflower florets with the oil in a large bowl. Sprinkle with the salt and pepper, and toss to distribute the seasonings evenly.

Place the Cook & Crisp basket in the pot, press **Air Crisp**, set the temperature to **400°F (204°C)** and allow the Foodi to preheat for **5 minutes**. Place the cauliflower mixture in the basket (it's okay if they overlap), set the timer to **15 minutes**, then press **Start**.

When the time is up, toss the cauliflower with the Parmesan cheese and serve with marinara sauce.

JALAPEÑO POPPER POTATOES

SERVES 4

Functions Used
Air Crisp

1 lb (454 g) baby red potatoes, halved or quartered depending on their size

2 tsp (10 ml) extra-virgin olive oil

1 tsp coarse salt, divided

8 oz (227 g) cream cheese, softened

½ cup (110 g) sour cream

½ tsp garlic powder

¼ tsp black pepper

1 cup (121 g) shredded Cheddar or Mexican-blend cheese

2 green onions, chopped

2 jalapeños, stem and seeds removed, then finely chopped

½ cup (60 g) cooked and crumbled bacon

Tender, crispy potatoes are paired with a creamy, cheesy and slightly spicy topping, making these almost like Irish nachos, only better! Add chopped cooked chicken for a main dish or leave them as-is for an appetizer or side dish.

In a medium-sized mixing bowl, toss the potatoes with the oil and ½ teaspoon salt. Place the Cook & Crisp basket in the pot, press **Air Crisp**, set the temperature to **390°F (199°C)** and allow the Foodi to preheat for **5 minutes**.

Place the potatoes in the basket, set the timer to **18 minutes** and press **Start**. Shake the basket halfway through cooking time. Cook for 18 minutes, or until the potatoes are cooked through and crispy.

Meanwhile, in a mixing bowl with a spoon, mix together the cream cheese, sour cream, garlic powder, remaining salt, pepper and shredded cheese until well-blended and smooth. Spread the mixture over the crispy potatoes (it doesn't have to cover them completely). Still using the **Air Crisp** function, cook for **3 minutes**, then top with the green onions, jalapeños and crumbled bacon.

GREEN BEAN & BLUE CHEESE CASSEROLE

SERVES 6 TO 8

Functions Used
Sear/Saute, Bake/Roast

4 (14.5-oz [411-g]) cans green beans

2 tbsp (30 ml) extra-virgin olive oil

1 medium sweet onion, chopped

2 cloves garlic, minced

½ cup (120 g) butter, divided

2 tbsp (15 g) flour

1 pint (475 ml) heavy cream

½ cup (60 g) crumbled blue cheese, plus more for garnish

½ tsp coarse salt

¼ tsp freshly ground black pepper

1 cup (121 g) French-fried onions, chopped

1 cup (56 g) panko breadcrumbs

Every holiday, this is my vegetable contribution. I've had so many friends ask for the recipe I thought it was time to share it here! The topping is a combination of chopped French-fried onions and panko breadcrumbs, which is the perfect pairing for its creamy filling. I love that I can have my turkey or ham in the oven while making this side dish in the Foodi.

Place the green beans in a colander and allow them to drain thoroughly. Press **Sear/Saute** and set the heat to **Medium**. Allow the Foodi to preheat for **5 minutes**.

Add the oil to the pot and when it's shimmering, add the onion. Cook for about **5 minutes**, stirring frequently. Add the garlic and cook for **1 minute**. Add ¼ cup (60 g) of the butter to the pot and allow it to melt, stirring occasionally, about **2 minutes**. Sprinkle the flour over the butter mixture, then stir and cook with the flour for another **1 to 2 minutes**.

Slowly stir in the cream. Bring the mixture to a simmer, then add blue cheese and press **Stop** to turn off the Foodi. Stir the mixture until the blue cheese is incorporated (small pieces are fine). Stir in the salt and pepper. Add the green beans to the pot and gently mix until they're well-coated.

In a microwave-safe bowl, melt the remaining butter in the microwave. Add the chopped French-fried onions and breadcrumbs and toss them to coat. Sprinkle the mixture over the casserole in the pot. Close the crisping lid. Press **Bake/Roast** and set the temperature to **350°F (177°C)** and the timer to **15 minutes**. Press **Start**. When the time is up, open the lid and allow it to sit for **10 minutes** before serving. Garnish with some extra blue cheese crumbles if you'd like.

MEXICAN STREET CORN (ELOTE)

SERVES 6

Functions Used
Air Crisp

Oh, street corn, how I adore you! It's rare that I prepare corn-on-the-cob and don't serve it this way. Tajin seasoning is a chili-lime seasoning with a very unique flavor and can be purchased at most grocers and almost all Mexican grocery stores. It pairs wonderfully with the sweetness of the corn, but I use it on everything, especially fresh-cut fruit for a healthy snack. The combination of flavors and textures in this Mexican Street Corn is one I know you'll love!

6 ears corn, husked and cleaned

1 tbsp (15 ml) extra-virgin olive oil

⅓ cup (73 g) mayonnaise

⅓ cup (40 g) cotija cheese

1–2 tbsp (8–16 g) Tajin seasoning

1 tbsp (3 g) chopped cilantro (optional)

6 lime wedges, for serving

Brush the corn with the olive oil. Place the Cook & Crisp basket in the pot, press **Air Crisp**, set the temperature to **390°F (199°C)** and allow the Foodi to preheat for **5 minutes**.

Place 3 ears of corn inside the basket. Set the timer to **10 minutes** and press **Start**. Halfway through the cooking time, flip the corn. When the time is up, repeat the process with the remaining corn.

When all the corn has finished cooking, brush the mayonnaise all over each cob. Sprinkle evenly with the cheese and Tajin seasoning, then the chopped cilantro (if using). Serve with the lime wedges.

SWEET & SPICY ACORN SQUASH

SERVES 2 TO 4

Functions Used
Air Crisp

2 tbsp (30 g) butter, melted

2 tbsp (23 g) light brown sugar

1 tbsp (15 g) adobo sauce (from a can of chipotle peppers)

½ tsp coarse salt

1 large acorn squash, cut into quarters and seeds removed

This is how we ate our squash when I was growing up, and it's remained a favorite of mine! The addition of the adobo sauce is new, however, since I love the combination of sweet and spicy. Feel free to leave out the adobo sauce if you'd prefer; it's delicious and simple either way!

Combine the butter, brown sugar, adobo sauce and salt in a small dish. Brush the mixture all over the cut sides of the squash.

Place the Cook & Crisp basket in the pot, press **Air Crisp**, set the temperature to **375°F (191°C)** and allow the Foodi to preheat for **5 minutes**. Place the squash inside the basket. Set the timer to **20 minutes** and press **Start**. Cook the squash for **20 minutes**, or until it's fork-tender and lightly browned.

GARLIC PARSNIP FRIES

SERVES 4 TO 6

Functions Used
Air Crisp

The parsnip is an often-overlooked root vegetable that deserves its time to shine. The texture of parsnip fries is similar to regular fries but the flavor is so much better! The Foodi is the perfect way to make this delicious side or appetizer, since all you have to do is shake the basket to get perfectly crispy French fries. Having said that, feel free to use peeled russet potatoes if you prefer traditional French fries.

¼ cup (54 g) extra-virgin olive oil

2 cloves garlic, crushed

3 lbs (1.4 kg) parsnips, peeled and cut into strips about ½ inch (1 cm) wide

1 tsp coarse salt

¼ tsp freshly ground black pepper

Heat the oil and garlic in a small saucepan until it reaches a strong simmer. Keep it at a simmer for about **5 minutes**, stirring occasionally, then turn off the heat. Allow it to sit for **15 minutes**, then discard the garlic.

Toss the garlic oil with the parsnips. Place the Cook & Crisp basket in the pot, press **Air Crisp**, set the temperature to **390°F (199°C)** and allow the Foodi to preheat for **5 minutes**. Place the parsnips inside (it's okay if they overlap), set the timer to **20 minutes** and press **Start**. Every **5 minutes**, open the lid and shake the fries. Cook until they're cooked through and crispy. Season with the salt and pepper.

CHARRED BROCCOLI WITH GARLIC & PARMESAN

SERVES 4

Functions Used
Air Crisp

1 medium head of broccoli, divided into florets

1½ tbsp (22 ml) extra-virgin olive oil

¼ tsp salt

¼ tsp garlic powder

¼ cup (25 g) shredded Parmesan cheese

After I tried cooking broccoli in the Foodi for the first time, I knew I'd never prepare it another way. It gets perfectly charred, which adds a ton of flavor! There's no need for a sauce here, and even your pickiest eaters will gobble this up.

Toss the broccoli with the olive oil in a large bowl. Mix together the salt and garlic powder, and sprinkle it over the broccoli, tossing to coat it evenly.

Set the Cook & Crisp basket in the pot, press **Air Crisp**, set the temperature to **390°F (199°C)** and allow the Foodi to preheat for **5 minutes**. Place the broccoli mixture in the pot, set the timer to **10 minutes** then press **Start**.

When the time is up, open the lid and sprinkle with the Parmesan, tossing gently to coat.

BUTTERY HERBED CARROTS

SERVES 4

Functions Used
Pressure Cook

1 lb (454 g) carrots, peeled and cut into 1-inch (2.5-cm) pieces

½ cup (118 ml) chicken or vegetable broth or stock (or water)

¼ cup (60 g) butter, softened

1 tsp Herbs de Provence

½ tsp coarse salt

Herbs de Provence is an herb blend that's widely available at most grocers. It makes everything taste heavenly, especially carrots tossed with butter! If you prefer a lighter side dish, use 2 tablespoons (30 ml) of extra-virgin olive oil in place of the butter.

Place the carrots and broth in the pot. Place the pressure lid onto the pot and make sure the valve is set to **Seal**. Press **Pressure** and set to **HI**. Set the timer to **2 minutes**, then press **Start**.

When the time is up, carefully release the pressure by turning the valve to **Vent**. When all of the pressure is released, open the pot, drain all the broth from the pot and gently pat the carrots dry. Add the butter to the pot and gently toss it with the carrots until they're completely coated. Add the Herbs de Provence and salt, then toss gently just to combine.

BAKED SWEET POTATOES WITH MARSHMALLOWS

SERVES 4

Functions Used
Air Crisp, Broil

1 tbsp (15 ml) extra-virgin olive oil

2 large sweet potatoes
(or 3–4 small or medium-size)

½ tsp coarse salt

½ cup (25 g) mini marshmallows

Sweet potatoes and marshmallows might be a typical holiday dish, but the Foodi makes it so simple you can make anytime! Being able to both air-fry the potatoes and broil the marshmallows without having to turn on the oven means these aren't just for holidays anymore.

Brush the olive oil all over the outside of the potatoes. Place the Cook & Crisp basket in the pot, press **Air Crisp**, set the temperature to **390°F (199°C)** and allow the Foodi to preheat for **5 minutes**. Place the sweet potatoes inside the basket, set the timer to **40 minutes** and press **Start**.

Cook for **40 minutes**, or until the potatoes are soft and tender. Remove from the basket and place them on a cutting board. Carefully cut the potatoes in half, then sprinkle with the salt. Place the potatoes back in the pot. Top the potatoes with the mini marshmallows. Close the lid, press **Broil** and set the timer to **3 minutes**. Broil until the marshmallows are lightly browned.

PERFECT PEPPERS, MUSHROOMS & ONIONS

SERVES 4

Functions Used
Air Crisp

1 poblano pepper, stem and seeds removed, then sliced

1 red bell pepper, stem and seeds removed, then sliced

½ lb (227 g) button mushrooms, halved

1 medium onion, sliced

1 tbsp (15 ml) extra-virgin olive oil

1 tsp coarse salt

½ tsp freshly ground black pepper

This healthy side dish is so simple and goes with just about anything! Serve it alongside steak or chicken, add it to a salad or use it as a taco topping. The possibilities are endless!

Toss all of the ingredients together in a medium-sized mixing bowl.

Place the Cook & Crisp basket in the Foodi, press **Air Crisp**, set the temperature to **390°F (199°C)** and allow the Foodi to preheat for **5 minutes**. Place the vegetables in the basket, set the timer to **12 minutes** and press **Start**. Cook just until the vegetables are crisp-tender.

TEMPTING SWEETS

No cookbook would be complete without at least a few sweet treats, so I've included our tried-and-true recipes here. Who would have thought you could make fried donuts and bake a cobbler with the same machine? A few of these recipes even double as an indulgent breakfast, so don't wait until after dinnertime to enjoy them!

My Three Favorites

CARAMEL MONKEY BREAD

SERVES 4 TO 6

Functions Used
Bake/Roast

Cooking spray
¾ cup (150 g) sugar
1½ tsp (4 g) cinnamon
2 (16.3-oz [462-g]) cans
buttermilk biscuits
1 cup (220 g) firmly packed
brown sugar
¾ cup (180 g) butter or
margarine, melted
¼ tsp coarse salt

Note: Since this dish can get a little messy, make sure to clean or soak your pan right away to help with cleanup.

So easy your kids can make it? Check. Gooey, caramelly and melt-in-your-mouth delicious? Check! Bookmark this recipe for lazy Sunday mornings, the holidays or just because. It's that good!

Spray the Foodi pot lightly with cooking spray. Using a large resealable plastic bag, mix together the sugar and cinnamon. Separate each biscuit in half lengthwise by pulling them apart, then cut each half into quarters.

Add the biscuit pieces to the bag and shake to coat them with the sugar and cinnamon. It's helpful to put a few pieces in the bag, shake the bag a little and keep adding as you go to keep the dough from sticking together; do this in several batches. As you finish each batch, place the pieces in the greased pot.

In a small bowl or a glass measuring cup, mix together the brown sugar, melted butter and salt. Pour the mixture over the biscuit pieces. Close the crisping lid. Press **Bake/Roast** and set the temperature to **350°F (177°C)** and the timer to **25 minutes**. Press **Start**.

When the time is up, open the crisping lid but allow the monkey bread to cool in the pot for **10 minutes**. Remove the pot from the base, then turn it upside down onto a serving plate. Pull apart or slice into pieces to serve.

OVERNIGHT CARAMEL & BERRY FRENCH TOAST

SERVES 4

Functions Used
Bake/Roast

You know those recipes that are made so often in your family that they become tradition? This is one of those recipes for us. Not only is it absolutely delicious, but the fact that the prep is done the night before means all you have to do is wake up, turn on your Foodi and press start! You'll love the caramel-like coating on this delicious and simple French toast.

Cooking spray
5 large eggs
1 cup (237 ml) milk
1 tsp vanilla
¼ tsp salt
½ cup (120 g) butter
1 cup (220 g) brown sugar
2 tsp (10 ml) white corn syrup
¾ loaf (about ¾ lb [340 g]) French or brioche bread, sliced
1 cup (150 g) fresh raspberries, strawberries or blueberries (or a combination)

Grease the Foodi pot with cooking spray. Add the eggs, milk, vanilla and salt to a medium mixing bowl. Use an electric mixer to beat until smooth and frothy, about **2 minutes**. Set it aside.

On the stovetop, melt the butter, brown sugar and corn syrup in a medium saucepan. Bring it to a boil and, once boiling, stir constantly for **1 minute**. Pour the mixture into the greased pot, tilting the pot as needed to spread it to the edges. Place the bread slices on top, breaking them up as needed to fill in all the gaps.

Pour the egg mixture over the bread, pressing down to ensure all the pieces are soaked in the mixture. Cover the pot with plastic wrap or aluminum foil and refrigerate overnight.

Whenever you're ready for breakfast, take the pot out of the refrigerator, remove the plastic wrap or aluminum foil, and place the pot in the Foodi. Close the crisping lid. Press **Bake/Roast** and set the temperature to **350°F (177°C)** and the timer to **35 minutes**. Press **Start**. When the time is up, invert the French toast onto a serving platter, then top with the fresh berries.

CINNAMON & SUGAR DONUTS

SERVES 4

Functions Used
Air Crisp

1 can (16.3-oz [462-g]) flaky biscuit dough
2 tsp (5 g) ground cinnamon
½ cup (100 g) sugar
Pinch of coarse salt (optional)
Cooking spray
2 tbsp (30 g) butter, melted

I've been making these "donuts" as long as I can remember! When I started using my Foodi, I was so happy that I no longer needed to fry them the traditional way. These easy, delicious donuts are far less messy to prepare but every bit as tasty! Reserve any extra dough for another recipe or simply fry it up as donut holes.

Separate the biscuit dough and, using a small circle cutter, cut out the middle of each biscuit. Mix together the cinnamon, sugar and salt (if using) in a shallow dish. Place the Cook & Crisp basket in the pot, press **Air Crisp**, set the temperature to **375°F (191°C)** and allow the Foodi to preheat for **5 minutes**.

Spray the basket with cooking spray, then place the donuts inside in a single layer (do this in batches). Set the timer to **5 minutes** and press **Start**. When the time is up, remove the donuts, brush them lightly with melted butter and coat them in the cinnamon-sugar mixture.

BOURBON PEACH HAND PIES

SERVES 6 TO 8

Functions Used
Air Crisp

3 ripe peaches, peeled and diced

3 tbsp (45 ml) bourbon

3 tbsp (23 g) flour

¼ cup (50 g), plus 3 tbsp (38 g) sugar, divided

¼ tsp salt

2 prepared refrigerated pie crusts

1 large egg yolk

1 tbsp (15 ml) water

Peaches and a little bourbon are heavenly, but when you pair that with a tender, flaky pie crust it's even better. These little pockets of sweet deliciousness are the perfect way to use those summer peaches!

Mix together the peaches, bourbon, flour, 3 tablespoons (38 g) of sugar and the salt in a medium-sized bowl.

Gently unroll the pie crusts onto a floured work surface. Using a 2-inch (5-cm) circle cutter, cut out small circles from the pie dough (any size will work, just use more filling if you make them larger). Place about 1 teaspoon of peach filling into center of a circle. Lightly wet the edges of the dough with a small amount of water, then fold the circles in half and seal them with the tines of a fork. Mix together the egg yolk and water, then brush the top of the pies with the mixture. Sprinkle the pies with the remaining sugar.

Place the Cook & Crisp basket in the pot, press **Air Crisp**, set the temperature to **350°F (177°C)** and allow the Foodi to preheat for **5 minutes**. Place the pies inside the basket in a single layer (do this in batches). Set the timer to **12 minutes** and press **Start**. Bake the pies until they're golden brown, adding another minute or two if necessary.

SUGAR & HONEY CHEESECAKE BARS

SERVES 6 TO 8

Functions Used
Bake/Roast

3 (8-oz [226-g]) packages cream cheese, softened

1 cup (200 g) sugar

1 egg

1 tsp vanilla extract

Cooking spray

1 (8-oz [226-g]) can crescent rolls

½ cup (120 g) butter, melted

¾ cup (150 g) sugar

1 tsp cinnamon

Honey, for topping

The crunchy cinnamon-and-sugar topping on these cheesecake bars makes this dessert delightfully addicting! And using crescent rolls for the crust makes them easy to make. They're a great ending for a Mexican-themed meal or just for any time, because they're so good!

Using a hand or stand mixer, beat together the cream cheese, sugar, egg and vanilla in a medium-sized bowl until the mixture is smooth.

Line the bottom and sides of the pot with foil, high enough up the sides that the cheesecake will be able to be pulled out of the pot after baking. Spray the foil with cooking spray. Unroll the crescent roll dough and divide it in half. Place one half on the bottom of the pot, stretching it if necessary and crimping the perforated seams together. Spread the cream cheese mixture over the crescent roll dough. Place the second half of the dough over the cream cheese mixture, pinching the perforated seams together.

Mix together the butter, sugar and cinnamon. Pour it over the crescent roll dough in the pot and gently spread to cover completely. Close the crisping lid. Press **Bake/Roast** and set the temperature to **350°F (177°C)** and the timer to **30 minutes**. Press **Start**. Bake until it's browned and cooked through (the butter topping should be almost "dry" when it's done).

Remove the pot from the Foodi and allow the cheesecake to cool completely to room temperature. Using the foil as handles, lift the cheesecake out of the pot, then cut into bars. Drizzle with the honey before serving.

FRESH PEACH COBBLER

SERVES 6 TO 8

Functions Used
Bake/Roast

½ cup (90 g) brown sugar

½ cup (60 g) all-purpose flour

½ cup (40 g) rolled oats

½ tsp cinnamon

Large pinch of salt

¼ cup (30 g) chopped pecans

¼ cup (60 g) unsalted butter, cut into 16 cubes

6 peaches, peeled and cut into 8 slices each (about 3 cups [462 g] sliced peaches)

½ tsp lemon zest

1 tbsp (15 ml) lemon juice

1 tbsp (9 g) cornstarch

¼ tsp vanilla extract

Cooking spray

Vanilla ice cream, for serving (optional)

The crunchy topping with pecans on this cobbler is what makes it special, despite that it's so simple to prepare. Try adding a cup of fresh raspberries for a delicious flavor twist.

In a small bowl, mix together the brown sugar, flour, oats, cinnamon, salt and pecans. Add the butter and, using your fingers or a fork, pinch or cut the butter into the mixture until the butter is the size of peas. In a separate large bowl, mix together the peaches, lemon zest and juice, cornstarch and vanilla.

Spray the Foodi's multipurpose pan with cooking spray and set it on the trivet inside the Foodi. Place the peach mixture in the pan. Sprinkle the topping evenly over the peach mixture.

Close the crisping lid. Press **Bake/Roast** and set the temperature to **390°F (199°C)** and the timer to **30 minutes**. Press **Start**.

Bake for **30 minutes** or until the top is golden brown and the cobbler is hot and bubbling. Serve warm or at room temperature, with vanilla ice cream if you'd like.

ACKNOWLEDGMENTS

I'm incredibly fortunate to have wonderful people in my life to help cheer me on during good times and bad. This is my fifth book and I may sound like a broken record, but a few words will never convey my appreciation and gratitude for you:

My parents, Art and Joyce Heppner, who are the kindest, hardest-working, most incredibly funny and delightful people around. You stood by me when things weren't easy and have been endlessly supportive. My favorite place on earth is your back porch, which is always safe, comforting and filled with laughter. I love you so, so much!

My daughters, Kylie and Katie, who are fiercely independent, strong, kind and hilarious teenagers and who I'm crazy proud of. You have each followed your own path, and I know you will do great things. You bring so much joy to my life, and I'm very proud to be your mom!

My funny, crazy, hardworking and always thoughtful partner, Rob Wadsworth. Thank you for always believing in me and always doing whatever you can to make our life together easy, fun and filled with so many laughs!

My dearest friend, Lara Nesbit, who wins the hearts of everyone she meets. You're the epitome of class and elegance mixed with sass and grace. I love you always.

To my dear friends who keep me laughing and grateful because you're just so amazing . . . thanks for coming along on this journey with me.

As always, thanks to the Page Street Publishing team for your support. You're the best!

ABOUT THE AUTHOR

Kristy Bernardo is the creator of the popular food blog The Wicked Noodle and has been an influential member of the food blogging world for more than twelve years. Although mostly self-taught, she has been strongly influenced by her mother and grandmother and honed her skills at boot camp at the Culinary Institute of America in Hyde Park, NY. She has owned a successful business as a personal chef, has taught cooking classes to all ages, speaks at conferences and events and has appeared regularly on video and television. She is the author of *Weeknight Cooking with Your Instant Pot, Cooking from Frozen in Your Instant Pot, Weeknight Keto* and coauthor of *The Big Book of Instant Pot Recipes*. Kristy lives in northern Virginia with her partner, Rob, and her daughters, Kylie and Katie. You can most often find her walking or biking the nearby trails, creating in her kitchen or trying new cocktails at restaurants everywhere.

INDEX